PRAISE FOR GEMS OF DELIGHT

"Lisa McCrohan has so much to teach the world about living intentionally with compassion for self and others. In *Gems of Delight*, Lisa's deep wisdom is woven into poetic passages and stories from her life. Her voice is nurturing, encouraging, and uncomplicated, like a wise and faithful friend to turn to when the world is loud and hurtful. Lisa gently reminds us to turn inward and look upward to find what our souls need to thrive. With just one short reading a day, *Gems of Delight* will remind you why life must be lived moment by moment, heart to heart, hand in hand."

—Rachel Macy Stafford, New York Times bestseller author of *Hands Free Mama, Hands Free Life,* and *Only Love Today*

"In her kind and honest way, Lisa McCrohan invites readers to reconnect with that which truly nourishes them: their inner truth, the present moment, the power of compassion, even the changing seasons. This is a book readers can return to time and again."

—Carla Naumburg, Ph.D., author of *Parenting in the Present Moment*

"Lisa's words are salve for the woman's soul. The poetry alone is worth holding this book in your hands and never letting go, but her stories, her insights, and her prompts are delicious and powerful. This is the one book you'll want to pick up for yourself—and for a friend or three."

—Shawn Fink, Founder, The Abundant Mama Project

"*Gems of Delight* is a well of nourishment and a gift of encouragement. Lisa's words call to the authentic self, reminding us that living in gratitude, honesty, and divine connection transforms the little and big worlds we inhabit. In a culture where we are expected to be so many things, *Gems of Delight* reminds us that our most important job is to be our beautifully-messy, delightfully-complicated, life- and light-giving selves."

—Anne Hofmann, MEd, MA, Assistant Professor of English, Frederick Community College

"*Gems of Delight* is the result of a life-long exploration of the Sacred. It is a powerful personal and mindful parenting resource filled with the same touchstones and meditations, beautiful artwork and mystical poetry that have come to hang on my walls and have woven deeply into my spiritual fabric of understanding. Lisa has infused each page and word with her playful explorations of the mystical, practical, and intellectual, creating a healing balm that inspires delight, ease, and compassion in everyday life."

—Jenn Wilhelm, MS, OTR/L, Child and Family Occupational Therapist

"In this culture of hurry and striving, Lisa McCrohan's beautiful collection of *Gems* is a gentle yet powerful guide to healing. Her words eloquently come together to support and encourage embracing a more intentional and meaningful life. Lisa's wisdom and authenticity invite you to slow down and join her on a soul nourishing journey through the seasons, toward greater compassion, connection and delight."

—Erin U. McKinney, MSW, LICSW, CMHS, Psychotherapist, Child Mental Health Specialist

"Beautiful, comforting words from a loving, compassionate woman. Reading this book, filled with so many gems, fills my heart and makes me smile. I can hear Lisa's encouraging voice on every page, in every prayer and poem. Gorgeous words of encouragement for every season and every mood, for moms everywhere."

—Molly Fellin Spence, writer, editor, and co-owner of Spence Photographics

"Just like a diamond passing through fire survives and becomes more brilliant, we as human beings need gems to support us in both good and difficult times. Lisa's words are good medicine – deeply healing medicine which we all need."

—Ali Guida Smith, LMFT, Healing Arts Peace Projects

"*Gems of Delight* allows women to see themselves through the soft eyes of compassion. Lisa guides us to slow down, notice, feel, and express the Divine Feminine within. This is powerful word medicine given in gentle doses."

—Amber Santosha Sparks, RYT200, Author of *Heart Wanderings: Poetry of Love, Loss, and Light*

"*Gems of Delight* is insightful, authentic, filled with everyday experiences of faith in God and a wealth of wisdom. Lisa McCrohan eloquently shares her life experiences as a woman, wife and mother along with professional expertise as a social worker and counselor to encourage people to draw closer to God and enjoy the abundance of God's blessings throughout the seasons of life. I wholeheartedly recommend reading *Gems of*

Delight over the course of a year and to give as a gift to friends and family."

—Stacey M. Winston, Communications Specialist for Humanitarian Affairs, United Nations

"*Gems of Delight* is a treasure trove of wisdom. Lisa strives to connect with God and others and poetically gives voice to the spirit within each of us that is often ignored. In an era of hurry and a culture that runs skin deep, this book provides insightful guidance on nurturing a more intentional pace of life that allows us to delve deeper to become more authentic and loving people."

—Laura Lee Nation, JD, Attorney

"Are you ready to let your deep inner well of delight bubble up and spill out to your little corner of the world? Between the covers of this book lies a gentle guide to get you there. With each lovingly written word, you will feel nourished, safely-held, and aligned with your truest self. Lisa's vulnerable writing style will touch your heart in a profound way, and lead you on the path to becoming a more compassionate, unhurried mama."

—Denise Castner, mom, wife, & sower of kindness

"It is rare to come across an individual as devoted to the inner journey as Lisa McCrohan. In these times, we need her words, her soulful, soothing inspirations, more than ever. *Gems of Delight* is an invitation to go within and discover the places in you that have been calling out and beckoning you near. Breathe deeply, go slowly and heed the call—we need your spirit to come forth as well."

—Meghan Nathanson, Mindfulness Writer & Artist

"Lisa' s poetry and spirituality in *Gems of Delight* capture in a contemporary world, the deep feelings women have had for generations. Her beautiful words make sacred the everyday joys and challenges of being woman, mother, and wife. Her prayers, meditations and challenges are a gift and a true celebration of feminine wisdom."

—Kay McCrohan, MFA, Artist, Lisa's Mother-in-Law

"Because I am Lisa's mother, I know that she has lived and breathed each word she writes in *Gems of Delight*. This book provides the reader with a soul-filled guide to living in sync with the energies of the seasons. Her invitation to prayer, personal reflections, and dynamic poetry will encourage you to live from the heart. Lisa's authentic voice supports and accompanies the reader as a dear friend, giving you permission to 'say yes to the invitation of your soul'."

—Mary Ann Ackerman, Lisa's mom

Gems of Delight

seasonal inspirations for moms to heal the hurry and embrace what is sacred

LISA MCCROHAN

Lisa McCrohan

Cover design by Pixelstudio.

Author photo by David S. Spence.

Year of the Book
135 Glen Avenue
Glen Rock, PA 17327

ISBN 13: 978-1-945670-12-1
ISBN 10: 1-945670-12-6

Library of Congress Control Number: 2017936087

Dedication

To Brian, Aidan, and Clara – you are my delights.

Acknowledgments

My writing (and my life!) have been an experience of the power of community. I would like to acknowledge the support and contributions of the many people who have helped make *Gems of Delight* a reality:

To my parents, Bob and Mary Ann; my siblings and sister-in-law, Jason, Rebecca, Julie, and Mike; my in-laws, John and Kay; and my dear friend, Shannon Borros; for your constant love, devotion, and belief in me. Thank you for encouraging me to always follow what delights my heart.

To the G.o.D. Squad for your amazing support in helping me launch this book and spread its message of delight.

To my Linger Here Community for the encouragement you give me and each other as we build a more compassionate world.

To my Frederick community for your daily accompaniment and friendship, especially Judy Bazis, Jenn Wilhelm, Rachel Johnson, Jenn Kmiecik, Julie Henderson, Chrissy Miller, Molly Spence, Suzanne Rosen, Lynne Griffin, Anne Hofmann, and my Sacred Timeout community.

To Julie Berrett-Abebe, Maria DiLorenzo, Ami Hernandez, Susan Hurley, and Cynthia Kennedy, my Boston College graduate school community of spiritual women who see, love, and accompany each other through all seasons of life.

To my fellow authors, Rachel Macy Stafford, Shawn Fink, Carla Naumburg, Amber Santosha Sparks, Meghan Nathanson, and Ali Guida Smith for your soulful writings and for encouraging me to bring my writing into the world.

To Rachel Van Tassel of Birchtree Marketing who has designed and maintained my website since day one.

To Caroline Leibowitz of LDesigns for the beautiful design of the Lisa McCrohan lotus logo.

To Tommy D'Aquino for producing an incredible promotion video for the Kickstarter Campaign.

To Demi Stevens of Year of the Book for her patient guidance in editing Gems of Delight and bringing these messages to print.

To Jennifer Leach and Keith Conley who passed away during the writing of this book and who taught me that we are the miracles in everyday life.

To Brian, Aidan, and Clara. Brian, you are the kindest human being I know. Your devotion to loving us, and your compassion for the world inspire me every day. Aidan, you have the spirit of a "go getter" in life. The tender ways you love all creatures and the zest you have for living inspire me to risk following what delights my heart and loving this world with compassion. Clara, the day you were born, you brought a new sense of delight into my life. Your art, prayers, songs, and smile make my heart smile.

My deep gratitude goes out to all the supporters of my Kickstarter campaign for their help in making this book a reality.

I would like to offer a special thank you to the following people for their generous support:

Mary Ann & Bob Ackerman	Jennifer A. Long
Tammy Elizabeth Antilla-Lowe	Erin McKinney
Shannon Borros	Johanna Mitchell
Rachel Bridges	Nicole Mitchell
Rosemary and Ted Brooks	Neil Roed
Denise Castner	Rachel Macy Stafford
Christina Collazo	Denise Trach
Maria DiLorenzo	Janice Ueda
Mary Lou Fisher	Rachel VanTassel
Cynthia Kennedy	Charlene Winegardner
Patricia Kreke	Sean, Christie and Deirdre

Your belief in this project and your generosity are deeply appreciated.

Contents

Introduction i
Blessing of Delight x

Winter

The Invitation of Winter 3
My Word for the Year 7
Love Starts Here 9
God Whispers 13
I Don't Want to Hurry 15
Grace Meets Us 17
You Don't Have to Do Anything to be Loved 21
Hold Only What Matters 23
It's Time to Come Inside 27
Cultivating Quiet 31
Spaciousness 33
Right Effort 35
One Delight a Day 37
Be Ready to be Surprised 41

Spring

The Invitation of Spring 45
Open to Possibility 49
Today I Am Going to Believe 51
Doing Less 53

The Invitation 57

Birthing...61

Noticing Signs 65

Everyday Resurrection 69

Sharing in Vulnerability 73

Modern-day Meeting at the Well...........................77

When Others See Us..81

The Call to Embodied Freedom 85

It's Time Now..87

One Glorious First Step..91

Summer

The Invitation of Summer..................................... 97

Stay and Soften.. 103

Regard... 107

Linger... 111

The Fullness of Now.. 115

Begin Again... 117

Love Looks 121

Holding Love 125

The Wildness Within 129

Orienting Toward Pleasure 135

Love Lists.. 139

Make Time for Joy.. 143

A Speck of Stardust.. 145

What Remains 151

Fall

The Invitation of Fall 157

Mindful Moments 161
Reclaiming the Sabbath 165
Embodying Sensuality..............................167
Radical Tenderness 169
Notice the Good...171
The Depth of Devotion 175
The Grief that Won't Go Away 179
Accept Support..185
Letting the Responsible One Rest............187
Forgiveness...189
Tiny Gifts that Matter 193
Yes to the Mess 199
A Sacred Revolution 205

Conclusion.. 209
A True Happiness 211

Introduction

The Hand of the Beloved

My Darling,
how is it that you search for Me like
a poor beggar on hands and knees, frantically
scrounging the dirt floor for food?
My Dear Heart, if you wish, I can continue
to beg and scrounge alongside you, and
we can keep bruising our hands and knees,
never really filling our bellies on the scraps
this world happens to toss our way.
But wouldn't it be easier
and a lot less on our hands and knees and hearts
to take the hand of the Beloved who
has always been holding such sweet
nourishing delights to
your parched lips?
Come, let's rest for a while.
Let's go outside and
lay under the vast moonlit night.

It's Mother's Day. We've had a full day of handmade gifts from my children and visiting my parents. We've also had squabbles, tiredness, and misunderstandings. We're on the highway returning home and I'm noticing how "quietly whole" I feel. Though nothing is perfect, I'm okay with that. Gentleness has taken root in me. I realize that life is both messy and miraculous. Sitting in the car – stuck in traffic, looking at my husband, looking at my children – I notice it: I'm not scrounging anymore.

When I became a mother, I scrounged for control. I scrounged for connection in a harsh and disconnected world. I scrounged to feel like I was enough.

A move to a new town, a tough pregnancy, a long labor that ended in a Cesarean section, and the shock of healing while caring for a newborn almost broke me. But I carried on. Then finally one day, while pushing my son in the stroller uphill in the cold and rain, alone, and utterly exhausted, I broke.

The cold wind and rain pelted my face while baby slept and I wept. My cries were uncontrollable. A neighbor drove past and later said I was crazy for being out on such a cold day. But I hadn't even seen her. All I saw was my brokenness. All I heard were my cries and the splash of stroller wheels on wet pavement. All I knew were my desperate prayers.

Then, in the midst of walking and weeping, I heard God gently whisper to me, *"Lisa, I'm here. I just want to be alongside you."*

That's the day I heard the holy invitation to go about motherhood in a way that was radically different from what our mainstream culture promotes.

~ I would base my everyday life on what was most sacred to me.
~ I would nourish myself with compassion and deep regard.
~ I would "listen within" to embody my feminine power, sensuality, and truth.
~ I would pause to truly see my children's light and empower them to be a compassionate presence in this world.

Slowing down would nourish me and my family. Learning to "listen within" would be our guide. Honoring the truth within me would be my compass. Compassion and love would lead us. Delight, beauty, and connection would save us. Embodying my feminine, sensual self would awaken my power.

What did I do?

I began to take Sacred Pauses. These little moments of getting grounded and reconnecting to my heart became my saving grace. They resourced me to respond instead of react. They became my gentle daily reminder to soften and go gently. They became the sacred space where I lingered with my children and really saw and regarded them.

I began to connect to a God of Compassion. I journaled with God. The "messy and miraculous" of daily life became my meditation cushion. "Listening within" taught me the power of kindness in a harsh world. As I connected to a God of Compassion, my capacity to have compassion for myself and others deepened.

I began to care for myself in deep, nourishing ways. I gave myself permission to invest the time, energy, and money in my own healing. I began to more deeply embody my sensual, feminine power.

I began to make decisions based on what was most sacred to me and my family. I made "big" decisions like leaving my full-time position at Georgetown University and "everyday" decisions like making time to cuddle in the morning.

Slowly, over many years, I am scrounging less. That quiet wholeness remains, along with a deeper sense of ease. Though I am far from perfect, I'm not trying for "perfect" anymore. I'm practicing embracing delight, extending compassion, and creating connection. My favorite mystical poet, Hafiz, said, "One regret dear world, that I am determined not to have when I am lying on my deathbed is that I did not kiss you enough." I want to spend my life kissing my dear ones and filling this world with delight and compassion.

Ten years ago, on that cold and rainy day, I chose to go about motherhood in a radically different way than our culture of hurry and quick fixes. Slowly, day by day, I have chosen to take the hand of the Beloved to linger, go gently, and love. My days now align with what is most sacred to my family. And I am devoted to the call within me to be a source of delight and compassion for my family, my clients, and this world.

I want this for you, too! And it's possible. That same hand of the Divine is outstretched to you. Yes, you can live your everyday life according to what is most sacred to you. You can heal the hurry. You can tap into your inner vibrancy and let it shine. You can have more capacity to see the light in your dear ones and be a presence that lets it shine brighter. You can connect more deeply. You can embrace your sensual, feminine power. An inner sense of freedom and spaciousness awaits.

In *Gems of Delight*, I share selections from my private journals, conversations with God, and honest expressions of my heart to help you journey from busyness to pausing, from harshness to compassion, and from brokenness to connection. These gems guide you into the inner landscape of your own heart. They help you take hold of the hand of the Beloved and live with clear focus and deep devotion to what is most sacred to you.

I designed this book with short gems so you could pick it up, turn to any page, and find inspiration at any time, in any season. With 52 gems, this book can also be your weekly guide to connect throughout the year.

You'll notice that I use "God language." I come from a Catholic background and have studied Christian theology, yoga, Buddhist meditation, Sufi spirituality, and various healing modalities for over two decades. Throughout this book, I use different words for the Divine – like Spirit, Beloved, and God. Choose the language that best resonates for you. God is bigger than labels.

I arranged *Gems of Delight* into seasons. Aligning our rhythm with the seasons connects us to our inner landscape. It grounds us to attune our senses to the pulse of the earth. It is how our ancestors lived for centuries. To honor the seasons is to reclaim this ancient wisdom and bring a deeper sense of ease to our day. We heal the disconnect. We discover a tremendous wellspring of inner vibrancy. And we live in rhythm with the Divine.

There is a sacred invitation in each season. Winter invites us to rest and lay fallow. Spring invites us to notice what wants to be birthed. Summer invites us to delight in play. Fall invites us to visit our own grief, practice forgiveness, and cultivate gratitude. Each season in this book contains five different types of entries:

~ Journal entry
~ Reflection
~ Conversation
~ God talks, I listen
~ I talk, God listens

"Journal entries" come from my own personal quiet time. "Reflections" come from my blog posts, workshops, sessions with clients, and sacred moments from everyday life as a family. "Conversations" are times God and I talked. And the "God talks, I listen" and "I talk, God listens" are times when one of us had something to say while the other one listened! For each entry there is a prayer and invitation to support you.

My life's work is about accompanying people to base their everyday lives on what is most sacred to them and feel the freedom that awakens when they live this way. I support people to live with a deeper sense of delight, compassion, and connection in simple, nourishing ways. I believe this is how we inspire a more compassionate world.

It is my hope that these gems help you reconnect to what is sacred to you, and to sense a God of Compassion alongside you in the messy and miraculous. Together, we can move from harshness to compassion, busyness to pausing, and discord to connection. I'm alongside you!

Blessing of Delight

May the gems in this book encourage you to slow down and pause in a busy world.

May you connect to a God of Compassion and feel the gentle presence of the Divine Within alongside you in the messy and miraculous of everyday life.

May God delight you, nourish you, and renew your inner sense of vibrancy.

May you reconnect to what is sacred in your day and find the gems within you, your life, each other, and our world.

May you awaken to your inner truth, sensuality, and power as you rise with clarity and devotion.

Together, may we make time for connecting with our own hearts, our dear ones, and others. May we uplift, encourage, and accompany each other in the joys and sorrows of life.

Together, may we heal the harshness and judgment we have with ourselves and each other through our compassionate presence.

As we live with clarity and devotion to what is sacred to each of us, may our presence revolutionize motherhood and create a more compassionate world.

Winter

The Invitation of Winter

The Temple Inside of Me

I sat and
became a
temple
Ten thousand visitors
came to see me –
grief, loss,
loneliness,
despair,
joy,
peace –
and I learned to
just sit
and receive them all
with kindness,
welcoming them as
I would
my Beloved.

It can be scary to slow down and step out of the busyness of everyday life. When we slow down and get quiet, we see what we have been avoiding. It makes us uncomfortable to feel our worries, fears, tiredness, disappointment, longings, and anger.

Yet there is a gentle, skillful way to press the pause button. Winter is a perfect time to slow down and linger. Winter calls us inside – inside our homes and inside our own self.

This winter can be an opportunity to pause and turn inward to deeply nourish yourself and connect with the Divine Within. This season offers an invitation to treat yourself as a temple, a sacred place for the indwelling of the Divine. The invitation is to listen to your body and honor what it needs – like rest, laughter, and healthy food. The invitation is to sit by candlelight and give your heart the space to speak to you. The invitation is to sense what needs healing, tending to, and nourishment.

It's countercultural to pause. It's countercultural for a mom (or any human being!) to say, "*Wait a second! No more! I am not going to run myself ragged. I'm done operating on empty.*"

It takes courage to say, "I'm going to focus on nourishing *me* and loving myself with such regard that such fullness and abundance flows to my family, too."

It takes courage to say, "I will tend to myself by finding the resources and support I need to live my life based on what is most sacred to me."

The truth is, you have a precious life to embrace and live. And there comes a time when you will not live it exhausted, holding up the world, stuffing down what needs to be healed within you, and ignoring the wisdom of your heart and body. The truth is each of us has an inner vibrancy that has been dulled by the pace at which we go about our days. The truth is we need to pause in order for this inner vibrancy to shine once again. Our spirits need spaciousness to breathe. And it begins with a radical, countercultural commitment to deeply nourish yourself.

Can you sense how it would be to live, parent, work, and love from a place of deep nourishment? Can you imagine how it would be to treat yourself as a temple? Can you sense how it would be to feel aligned with the Divine Within and living from a sacred space?

It's possible.

Say "yes" to the invitation of winter to rest, "go within," and explore the sacred landscape of the temple inside you. Say "yes" to the invitation of the Divine to learn how to bring presence and compassion to the "visitors" of grief, loneliness, longing, and joy… and welcome them all as beloveds. Say "yes" to living with a deeper sense of equanimity, clarity, and ease.

May these winter reflections support you as you deeply nourish yourself and honor the temple inside of you.

My Word for the Year

Journal Entry

It's January 1st. Everyone is still asleep as I lay here in the quiet. It's dark outside. The wind is blowing. I'm warm and comfy in my bed thinking about this new year. *Ahhhh*, a new beginning. I don't make any resolutions. I don't need a goal or a promise. I need a north star that will focus my heart and attention in a busy and harsh world. Something that is gentle yet powerful.

I put my hand on my heart and ask, "What's my word for the year, God? What word do I need to have on my heart and on my lips as I go about my day? What word needs to be my prayer, my focus, my touchstone as I make breakfasts, get backpacks ready, feed the dog, and sit at my computer to do work? What word will deeply nourish me? What word will open my eyes to see my partner as my beloved – a reminder that we are on the same team? What word needs to be my reminder of how I want to live this day and live this year when things aren't going the way I want them to, when tantrums happen, when the unexpected arrives, when old habits creep into my thinking and doing? What will be my word for the year?"

And then I listen. And I hear my word. I know in my gut this is it. I will carry it with me throughout the year, allowing it to change me. At the end of the year, I want to look back and see how this word has been woven within me, how I embodied it, day after day, carrying it with me and in my heart. I want to look back and see how my word has challenged me to redefine "strength" and to make mindful choices about how I go about my day, what I do with my time, and how I treat myself and others.

Prayer: God, please put a word on my heart that I will carry with me throughout the year. And as I go about my day, may this word take up residence within and challenge me in ways that my soul knows is for its own evolution. May my word for the year connect me to what is sacred. May it heal any harshness within me. May it open my heart to see all beings with compassion.

Invitation: Listen for your "word for the year." It may be one word or it may be a phrase. Then write it down and put it in a place you'll see it every day.

Love Starts Here

Love starts here –
gently placing your own hand on your heart,
feeling this breath as it arises – full or shallow –
and loving what is,
however it is,
within you.

And then, slowly, from such radical acceptance
love begins to flow again within you
and all around you
as abundant blessing
at the breakfast table, post office,
and commuter train.

Love starts here –
tenderly cupping your cheek with your own hand
the way your mom
or someone who cared for you very deeply
used to do –
or should have done –
gently holding all that arises
without judgment,
only tenderness
and spaciousness.

Love starts here –
in this moment, this choice,
to soften, open, and connect
to your breath
and your beloved,
feeling yourself finally
beginning to let go
and letting love in.

And then, slowly, from such radical compassion
kindness lights a path into the dark crevices
of your inner landscape.
The stone walls around your heart
begin to crumble,
revealing a soft, tender heart
that pulses with the light of the stars
and longs to breathe and shine
its light into this hungry world.

Reflection

People come to me in Somatic Psychotherapy and Compassion Coaching feeling lost and overwhelmed. Something holy within them is calling them to heal and grow. But they don't know where to start.

Whether we are talking about their parenting challenges, healing their marriage, grieving the loss of a parent, or following their passion, it always begins in the same place.

Love starts here – in this moment, noticing what is present right here within you as it arises, with kindness and acceptance. Love starts here – in the choice to turn toward yourself, gently place your hand on your own heart, and feel yourself breathing in and out, with the intention to welcome and love whatever arises, however it is, within you.

This is a radical place to start. It is not in the past spewing out details of old wounds. It is not in the future creating plans and strategies. It is not "outside yourself." The radical place to start is right here in this very moment with "cupping your cheek with your own hand, the way your mom or someone who cared for you deeply used to do – or should have done."

No matter what you are holding – an over-stuffed laundry basket or a broken heart – love must begin here with your own self. Maybe you have gone down the road of treating yourself harshly, going at it alone, trying to analyze your way to wholeness, or mending the brokenness through pushing yourself to do more, do it better, and make it perfect.

Love yourself into wholeness – with kind attention, tenderness, gentleness, and deep regard. I promise this "way of gentleness" will slowly begin to both soften and strengthen you. And the love within will begin to flow again all around you as abundant blessing to your dear ones and those you meet. The light of your heart will begin to brilliantly shine again – for your own self and for this hungry world.

Prayer: God, you call me to start with loving my own self. Giving such tender care to myself is new to me. Please remind me again and again to treat myself with kindness and deep regard. I am learning.

Invitation: A few times a day this week, cup your hand around your cheek, and just pause. Offer yourself kindness and tenderness, saying, "I see you, Dear Heart."

God Whispers

Conversation

Me: "God, I'm going to imagine YOU being alongside me as I go about my day. I'm going to imagine YOU whispering my 'word for the year' to me as a gentle, sweet invitation, because I am tired. I am tired of giving. I am tired of neglecting me. I am tired of going about my day in a culture of 'rugged individuals' and parenting like a mom who has to be it all and do it all."

God: "I see your tiredness, My Love."

Me: "I know that I am not the god to make it all happen. I feel alone and tired. I hold everything – from my children's wellbeing to the finances. The other day, a mom of four children said to me, 'I feel bad I'm not contributing financially to our family.' What?!! We are holding too much and expecting too much from ourselves."

God: "Yes, you are. I am alongside you, My Dear One. I love the image of me whispering your 'word for the year' as a gentle invitation. Yes, that's what it is. It is a reminder of who you really are. And I see, too, that you are feeling the waves of sadness and being alone now that Christmas is over, the holiday break is done, and the kiddos are back at school. You have so loved hanging with your family and friends. You have so loved being together, even when you are triggered and frustrated! And I know the quiet sadness you hold within you. These are such sweet times of connecting. You don't want them to end. I hear you, My Sweet Love."

Me: "I'm softly crying. I am used to carrying these emotions alone. So yes, this year, today, I'm going to imagine you beside me in my loneliness and tiredness. I'm going to imagine you whispering my word to me. I'm going to imagine this word taking root within me and connecting me to the truth of who I am. I am going to remember how deeply I am connected to you and to my dear ones."

Prayer: God of Compassion, you know how the holidays have been for me. You know the longings within me for deep connection. I'm going to imagine you walking beside me, sweetly whispering my 'word for the year' to me as we go about the day and confront the waves of emotions together.

Invitation: Imagine a compassionate God alongside you. Hear the Beloved whispering your 'word for the year' in a gentle, inviting tone.

I Don't Want to Hurry

I Talk, God Listens

Me: "Here I am, again, God, back to hurrying and back to feeling stressed to get everyone out the door! I'm so done with hurrying. I barked at my children. Even as I was telling them to hurry up, I couldn't believe my tone of voice. I saw the look of disappointment and hurt in their eyes. I saw their shoulders slump forward. What?! This is not me! And then I feel awful. How have we gotten stuck in this pattern?

"God, you know how good I am at time management. Yet I feel the pressure to hurry, like we have no time. I feel like I have to be on top of everything. I know, too, how it is for a nervous system to be stuck in 'stress mode.' I know how nerve-wracking it is to feel like there is no time.

"Is it me? Is it this culture? What do I do?

"God, help me to listen. I hear the call to slow down. Be with me. Show me how to slow down. I don't want to hurry. Help me to nourish my nervous system and my children's, too. Help me to treat my body as a temple – a holy place for the indwelling and expression of your Spirit."

Prayer: Dear God, I don't want to hurry anymore. Remind me throughout the day to slow down.

Invitation: This week, try taking a Sacred Pause – a nourishing moment of "coming home" to yourself and getting resourced. You can take just 30 seconds or three minutes of getting grounded and reconnecting to your heart, the Divine, and what matters most in order to go about your day with a deeper sense of intention.

Grace Meets Us

You are asleep in my arms, my precious little angel.
I linger in the silence, the dark, exhausted.
Even the soles of my feet ache.
There were moments today when I thought I'd lose it,
and moments when I did –
when I felt myself cracking open,
when I felt like a failure.
I'm too attached to "getting it right" –
believing that your outbursts mean
there's something wrong with me.
How many other women through the centuries
thought it was their fault,
that something was wrong with them?
God, how "mom" has taken the blame for too long now.
My nerves get so sensitive to the noise,
the sudden shifts of a four year old's mood.
And yet, now, here, you sleep.
The top of your head is in the crease of my elbow.
You are so peaceful now. You've let it all go.
Yet, I still hold the moments of the day too close.
"Let it go," I hear from within me.

And I see how tangled I am in this web of self-blame,
of taking too much responsibility, of trying too hard.
Here is the Divine's hand, reaching for mine
and I can simply take God's hand and step out.
The tangled mess in my mind loosens
and that's when Grace meets my willingness to
surrender.
It's all perfect,
a part of being human,
nothing to resolve or shift.
And I rest beside you now,
both of us,
free.

God Talks, I Listen

God: "You are sensitive because you are tired and holding too much. You can rest. You can let go of what just happened a moment ago (or ten years ago) and begin again right here, breathing in this moment – the softness of the covers, the rhythmic breathing of your daughter, and the warmth of her head against your arm. There is nothing wrong with you. Don't attach your sense of self to the changing moods of your children. They are their own persons. Let go of 'getting it right.' Instead just be human, be authentically you, and acknowledge the needs within you. Watch your little ones. See how they let Grace meet them right where they are! They begin anew in each moment, forgiving easily, letting go easily, and resting. I am here reaching out to you, always here to hold you, and for my Grace to flow through you."

Prayer: God, you call me to let your Grace meet me right where I am in my day – in my shame, in my "taking too much on," and in my desire to rest. You reach for my hand, asking me to surrender the negative beliefs I have about myself and to let your Grace wash over me so I can rest. I'm taking hold of your hand.

Invitation: Spend time this week watching a child. Notice how they don't let things bother them for too long. They move their bodies and "let it go." They sleep peacefully. Take some time to let your body move how it wants to and "let go." Then let their wisdom inspire you to rest, move in the way your body needs, and open to Grace.

You Don't Have to Do Anything to be Loved

God Talks, I Listen

God: "You don't need to *do* anything, My Love. You have been working so hard – your whole life. You are tired. That tiredness comes from believing it's all up to you, that you have to make it all happen. It comes from trying to 'make up for something.' It comes from the belief that you are not enough.

"You don't have to *do* anything. I will bring it all to your doorstep. You don't need to 'go out and make it happen' to prove anything or to atone for anything. You do not need to carry the world on your shoulders. Enough. Rest now. Delight in your everyday life. I will bring what you need to your doorstep.

"You can push me on this. It is hard to give up this habit of being so responsible and scared to let it all go and to trust. And yet, I will be beside you. I will teach you how to rest. I will show you how to delight in what your soul needs and your world needs. I will show you how my Grace turns the beliefs of this world upside down. True power lies in softening and allowing Love in. Let my message of ease, delight, and surrender take up residence in you."

Prayer: God, I hear you saying to me that I do not have to do anything to be loved. Period. I have held enough. But it is hard to let go of that belief. I am learning to believe that you promise me ease. I am learning to trust again.

Invitation: Pause and listen within. What message does the Divine Within have for you? How is God inviting you to see that you don't have to do anything to be loved? It takes time to let this radical kind of love wash over us and transform us. Keep coming back to the Divine's message of love for you.

Hold Only What Matters

Reflection

Today I was racing out with too many things in my hands and I shut the door. Instantly I knew I didn't have my keys. Crap. Should I call my husband? I knew that if he came back, he'd be late for an important meeting that he was facilitating. Neighbor? No one has our key. And I was running late.

I sat on the steps for a moment and started to tear up. *Pull it together, Lisa*, I said to myself. *What's the big deal?*

This is what we do when these moments of feeling broken arrive in our day, unplanned, and seemingly unprovoked. A word someone says sounds off-putting. A gesture your partner makes leaves you feeling "not seen." You drop off your kiddos at school and feel a quiet sadness swim across your heart. Then you say, "Pull it together," or "What's that all about?"

I called Brian. "I'll race back and open the door," he said.

But I didn't want him to race. I'm sick of racing. I don't want anyone to hurry. With my face in my hands, I heard from within me, *I'm holding too much.*

I paused. Yes, I'm holding too much.

How many of us hold too much? Too much trying to get it all perfectly aligned, the kiddos getting along perfectly, a perfect meal schedule for the week? How many of us hold too many commitments? How many of us hold too much of other people's stuff? How about running around too much?

The moment in which I saw I was holding so much, that inner voice, that whisper of deep truth that you can't deny, rose up from within and I heard her loud and clear: "Hold only what matters, Dear Heart. Hold only what matters."

Hold only what matters.

I am carrying way too much. I carry the anxiety for all of my family. I worry about everything. I hold it all. I feel the undercurrent of anxiety and an excessive responsibility for everyone's well-being. A rage is building within me. It comes out in moments when I am trying to do too much. I react. I am harsh. I see this in other moms, too. I'm carrying so much that I can't keep my arms around it all.

I see the overload and feel the weight of the burden in my head, heart, and arms. This stems from the loneliness and isolation of our culture. We as moms take on a brutal warrior posture – controlling and barking at our children, partner, and even another mom in her minivan at the stoplight.

I see how grasping for control is a way of avoiding my pain. Taking care of, and doing so much for others enables me to maintain a sense of control. It keeps me isolated because I don't share my needs. I don't allow others to hold me. Instead I carry everyone's load. Well, my back is breaking. Enough. I hear God calling me to hold only what matters.

What matters? Being true to my own heart. Pausing when my kiddos are around and looking at them. Letting go of old habits of relating, holding back, and feeling "I'm in this all alone and it's all up to me." Shining – yes, shining. Writing the poetry on my heart. Eating nourishing foods. Making time to talk with my mom. Honoring my body and taking a nap this afternoon. Moving my body. And slowing down.

This is holding only what matters. This is aligning the rhythm of my day with the seasons. This is honoring my truth and embodying my sensual expression. This is a day well spent that then becomes a lifetime devoted to holding only what matters.

Prayer: God, I am holding way too much. Show me how to hold only what matters.

Invitation: What if today you decided to "hold only what matters" and get rid of the other stuff? Dinner matters – but getting it perfect doesn't. Going grocery shopping matters – but doing it at a sprint doesn't. What if you started to make time for holding only what truly matters, like: pausing in your day; quitting the whole multi-tasking thing we are all addicted to; spending time just listening to your heart; and spending time just being with your dear ones? This week, keep the mantra "hold only what matters" close to your heart. Notice how it influences your thoughts, mood, actions, and interactions with others.

It's Time to Come Inside

God won't let me go looking for love
outside myself.
"It's time to come inside," she said.
"It's time to put your hand to your own cheek
and stroke your face with the gentleness of a mother
nursing her child.
No, I won't let you go looking outside anymore.
Come right here
and find me."

Conversation

Me: "God, I have worked with her for years in counseling. Today, sitting across from me, she finally began to feel the grief – named and unnamed. The grief clearly identified – like losing her mom – and the griefs that are harder to pinpoint which have shown up as disappointment, apathy, and frustration. They wanted to be acknowledged and tended to. For many years, we have been creating this sacred space to "go inside" with candlelight – not the harsh, glaring light of a spotlight.

We have been creating this safe place for her to learn how to clear away distractions and mindfully notice what is arising in her so she can respond with compassion. Instinctually she cupped her hand around her cheek. Ever so softly she began caressing and stroking her cheek. She was mothering herself with the gentleness she needed.

"This is how I imagine you want to be with us – holding us, mothering us with gentleness – right here in our holy bodies. How many times have I pushed that gentleness away? How many times have I pushed away those who love me?"

God: "Come right here and sit with me. Hear me calling to you. Find me here in the tending to, the creating space, and the listening to your body. Your body is the portal for deep love. It is holy. Find healing and a deep sense of contentment right here, through honoring your body with gentleness, sweetness, and compassion."

Me: "It's so simple. Pause. Turn inward. Be tender with myself. Yet our culture does not support such a posture! This world pulls me out of such sacred inner listening. Its messages are toxic to my inner landscape. And I bring these toxic messages into me – things like 'I'm not doing enough' and 'I'm not enough.' I'm done with it."

God: "Come and create this safe container within you. Come with candlelight. Come with gentleness. Cup your hand around your cheek. Let me mother you into wholeness."

Prayer: God, I hear you calling me inward. The pull of the world to look outside myself for happiness is strong. I want to come inside and allow myself to be mothered again.

Invitation: Ask yourself, "What kind of gentle mothering do I need from myself right now?" Is it tenderness? Kind words? Whatever it is, begin to offer this to yourself as you go through the week.

Cultivating Quiet

I Talk, God Listens

Me: "It's snowing outside. I feel the invitation to be inside, wrapped in a warm blanket and quiet. You call me inward to nourish myself with warm tea, hearty soups, quiet prayer, and rest. This month I am creating an at-home retreat. I want to listen to your voice and sense your healing presence.

"I'm giving myself permission to rest. I'm giving myself permission to take time out for me. I'm wearing clothing that makes me feel warm, comfortable, and sensual. I'm done overriding this desire to rest. I'm done trying to meet everyone's needs. I'm done putting my needs aside.

"I'm taking my life back. I'm taking my schedule back. And I am scheduling my self-care – like my quiet at-home retreat time and being with soul-nourishing friends. And I'm keeping it simple and doable.

"It's time that things come back into balance. It's time to honor the invitation of this winter season and deeply nourish myself. It's time I put caring for myself into my schedule and give myself permission for what truly nourishes me."

Prayer: God, I hear you telling me it is time to rest and be nourished. Help me to put my self-care on the schedule, just as I do with my children's activities and grocery shopping. It's time.

Invitation: Consider creating an at-home retreat. Set your intention to rest the senses, body, and mind. Wear warm, comfortable clothing that feels good on your body. Eat nourishing foods. And spend time reading a short inspiration each morning. Remember K.I.S.S. – keep it simple, sweetheart.

Spaciousness

The Way Home

I am quiet now.
Listening to my heart beat.
My breath leads me home.

Journal Entry

I am lying here on the floor near my desk, stretching and taking a break. A friend is picking up my daughter today from school. I have time to write, think, and stretch. I have needed such spaciousness, God. I have tended to our children and been present for them in the best way I know how and with all the love within me. It has been imperfect, but I have loved with all I have. And I see how we, as parents, need breaks! We need to tend to ourselves. We need spaciousness – quiet, undistracted spaciousness.

We need to slow our bodies down, rest against the earth, and listen to the beating of our hearts. We need the quiet spaciousness to listen to our breath and feel the breath leading us back to a deep sense of contentment and oneness – our Home. Here we remember how sacred our lives are. We remember our connections. We remember our place in the universe. We remember you, God, as the Holder, the Container of it all, our Home. This is how I want to live every single one of my days.

Prayer: God, keep telling me that it is more than "OK" to take breaks throughout the day! Keep drawing me into the quiet as I move away from the distractions of my day and come into stillness.

Invitation: This week, just once a day, can you turn off your phone, put the computer down, find a quiet space, and lay down on the ground? Can you listen to your heart beat and feel the breath moving through you? Whether it's for five breaths or five minutes, give yourself permission to pause and experience spaciousness.

Right Effort

Journal Entry

Maybe it's not time to "figure things out." Maybe it's time to just rest and listen. I can't help but notice that, right now, whatever I am trying to make happen and push along – putting lots of mental energy into – just doesn't go anywhere. It doesn't feel right. It's off. Yet I continue to "keep at it." I want to "figure it out" – *the* book I am to write, *the* offering I am to put out into the world, *the* way of explaining it all in writing. I know I'm forcing it and this is *not* working! I know this is not living aligned with the Divine.

The Beloved calls me to "right effort." I *know* what "right effort" feels like – it feels smooth, it has energy to it, nothing feels forced, my breath is slow and steady, my body is awake but not rigid or tight, and I feel a "yes" within me. When I am putting forth "right effort," I am honoring my body, my heart, and the season of my life.

"Right effort" feels like the place where Grace and I meet and we flow. That feels empowering and liberating. I have seen how "right effort" takes intention, discipline, and also kindness. And that takes pausing. That takes mindfulness.

Right now, in this season of my life, I know it is not the time to "keep at it" and "figure it out." I know God calls me to sit back, rest, and listen. My energies are "drawn closer in" – to being quiet, being with my family, and resting. I'm putting way too much energy into work. It's off balance. I know what I need to do. It's time to dance in such a way that I flow with God.

Prayer: God, you want to create a sense of ease in my life. Such ease arises from "right effort" on my part and trusting you. It's time that I let you lead this dance between you and me.

Invitation: This week, play with practicing "right effort." What does "right effort" feel like in your body? What is happening in your body when you are struggling for an answer, trying to figure something out, or you are putting forth a lot of effort? What happens when you ask for the Grace to flow with God's sense of ease? What do you notice happening in your body instead?

One Delight a Day

Journal Entry

What if God doesn't need me to *do* anything? What if I don't have to try harder, strive to be better, or even attempt perfection? What if a "sacred life" is really just an experience of drawing closer to the Divine? What if the Beloved couldn't care less about perfection and instead, is all about extending an invitation? An invitation to delight?

What if all God really wants of me is to experience delight? What if all God really wants is for me to see God abiding with me in any suffering, extending the invitation to feel Grace, comfort, and a renewed sense of delight in this life?

I write about the sacred in everyday life. I have done this since I was a little girl. Delight is an expression of the sacred that has been pushed out of our awareness and our day because we're going too fast, holding too much, and pushing too hard. God *is* delight. And when I am following what delights my heart, there is a deeper sense of ease, freedom, and connection within me.

I see now how delight doesn't discount my suffering. Actually, delight is a healing balm for my suffering. It allows my suffering to be here, too, and it shows me that pleasure and goodness are right here in my life to be experienced as a gift of hope even amid difficult times. Delight creates the sacred space within to remind me that Life and Love always find a way.

Such regard for delight invites me to rest! It invites me to drop the judgment and to soften. It invites me into relationship with the Divine.

No, I don't need to try harder or strive for anything. I don't need to fulfill a purpose or even become anything. The Divine is just inviting me to delight in this experience of being human and wants to be alongside me in it all. What a relief!

When I begin the day with the vow to notice just "one delight a day," inevitably this snowballs into noticing more and more delight. Simple delights. Everyday delights. Ordinary delights. Such noticing heals the overwhelm within me. I am more embodied. I feel the Beloved's holy invitation to experience how delight feels in my body – literally. My hips sway, my belly softens, and my spine undulates with soft, sweet, rhythmical movements. Delight is a soft light in the dark days of winter that lifts my mood, gently awakens my senses, and connects me to a deep vastness of Love that I recognize as Home. This is my true essence.

Prayer: God, you call me to notice one delight a day. Help me to believe it's possible that you don't call me to perfection or striving. You call me to soak up the simple delights of this human experience. And when I am suffering, you invite me to see you abiding with me, alongside me. Help me to hear your delightful invitation today.

Invitation: This week, begin your day with the vow to notice "one delight a day." Evoke the senses. Notice what delights your heart. Notice the tiny blessings. Notice God inviting you to cease the pursuit of perfection and instead savor the delights in your day. Notice how delight connects you to a deep vastness of Love that you recognize as your true Home.

Be Ready to be Surprised

Journal Entry

I'm up early this morning as my husband sets out to Connecticut for a funeral of a dear friend who lost his mom. It is still dark and I'm lying in bed, in the quiet. But my thoughts aren't quiet. They are all over the place. I am sad for people I know who have experienced tragedy this year. I feel the aches that people carry with them. Within my own self, I long for home as I sense the usual tug on my heart from visiting my family yesterday. Oh, how I wish they lived closer. For ten years now, I have longed for that. And today, this morning, God, I am feeling defeated.

"Look up," I hear.

So I look up. And just as dawn now appears through my bedroom window, I see our hibiscus – the one we dug up after the first frost hoping it would survive. The one that looked really bad but that I just kept watering and tending to for the last three months of winter. The one we put in our bedroom to get the best morning sun and the one I keep waking up to everyday and going to sleep to every night, sometimes shaking my head, sometimes sending it a little love, sometimes regretting that I wasn't "on it" quick enough to carry it inside before the first frost, sometimes just looking at it.

And there it is this morning – a beautiful orange-ish, red flower!

And I hear God whisper, "See, My Love. It's possible. Be ready to be surprised!"

I feel hope take root within me. I believe it's possible for hope to sprout in the most unlikely places. I'm ready to be surprised by you, God.

As winter ends and I welcome spring, I am reminded of your promise of hope. You will provide for me beyond what I can imagine and with abundance!

Prayer: God, I am ready to be surprised.

Invitation: Can you open your heart today and let God surprise you, to show you how hope blooms, and how the desires of your heart *are* possible?

Spring

The Invitation of Spring

Sacred Possibility

May you open to Sacred Possibility.
May you let go of efforting.
May you remember that you are
not the god to make it all happen.
May you slow down to allow the
wisdom of your body and spirit to
dance with the Divine's Grace that
brings you into sacred alignment
with what is holy and true to you.
May Sacred Possibility begin to
organically flow within you,
illuminating your inner vibrancy
so it shines in this world longing
for such light.

Spring calls us out of our homes and into the world. If winter invited us to look inward, spring now prompts us to look up and out. This is a season of hope, birth, and growth. We begin to see new life sprouting all around us.

Hope also sprouts. It grows and sends roots deep into the earth while at the same time reaching for the light. It can appear quite fragile – like a simple purple crocus blossom or fragile fruitless strawberry vines. But hope's root system is deep and tenacious. It breaks through rocks and mud to reach the light. Where hope is planted, it takes up residence. We may not see its "work" going on beneath the surface, but then one day, we notice that life is sprouting.

And when we see such life peek through what used to be barren landscape, something ancient within us remembers how hope is always here. We sense possibility! We see how the Divine has been here all along, breathing us into the next stage and planting seeds of hope. We sense that, somehow, our stories of "this isn't possible" and "it'll always be this way" are no longer true. We remember – deep in our bones – that life has a way of triumphing over death. Again and again.

These springtime reflections mirror the birthing process: from opening to the possibility of birth to saying "Yes"; from "I can't do this!" to "We are doing this!"; from gripping to letting go of control; from doubt to trust; and from what feels like death to resurrection. Whether we are birthing a child or a dream, we need others alongside us. We need faithful companions to remind us of what is possible. These reflections encourage us to reach out to soulful friends and build our tribe. Together, we stand, sing, dance, cry, and rejoice our way to life.

May these springtime reflections support you in giving life to what wants to be birthed from within you. May they encourage you to reach out to other like-hearted people to hold space for each other and the dreams you are about to birth.

Open to Possibility

God Talks, I Listen

God: "I know the doubts on your heart. You don't know how it could work out, how you could make it happen. It seems impossible. I know that winter has lasted too long. I know how you long for new life.

"My Love, have you forgotten who I am? I don't say this to be harsh. You know Me. I say this to remind you and bring comfort to you. I placed you in your mother's womb! I formed every fiber of your being. I placed this yearning within you. I placed my spirit within you.

"I called forth the winds from their slumber. I created the sky and the earth. I formed the sun and moon with my own two hands. I know the infinite vastness of the universes. I gave the robin her song and the wolf his howl. I formed the intricacies of your eyes and smile. There is nothing outside of me. I created it all.

"Imagine the furthest star your mind can grasp. And then multiply it by infinity. This is how far my love stretches for you. I intimately know each one of your ancestors and I know all who will come after you.

"And you think this dream, this hope, this yearning of yours is impossible?! Oh, My Love, look up at the heavens and see the reds, oranges, and purples of the sunset! Meditate on how I formed you and the stars!

"I want what you want! I want you to know happiness, to know freedom, and to be so very content. Please rest in this fact. Let me 'make it happen.' You, My Love, please just rest and tell yourself that I am making it possible."

Prayer: God, I have this deep yearning within me. I've had it for so long that right now, I am feeling like it's not possible. I will remember who you are, how you formed me, and how you love me. I know you are "making it happen" for me.

Invitation: As you go about your day, hear God's voice whispering to you, "I've got this. Please, just rest. Remember who I am. I know your desires. I know your heart. I will plant a deep sense of contentment in you."

Today I am Going to Believe

I Talk, God Listens

Me: "I am done spending my energy trying to change my dear ones. I am done trying to arrange circumstances just 'perfectly so.' Today I am going to believe that happiness is a choice – my choice. I am going to believe that I choose my inner experience, I choose the lens through which I look, and I choose my happiness.

"Today I'm going to believe that you exist even in the self-doubt, the unmet dreams, and the parts of me that feel lousy, insecure, crappy, and ashamed. I don't have to do anything to be holier or more loved.

"Today I'm going to believe that I don't have to 'go' anywhere to remember wholeness. Healing happens right here in this moment, arriving in this body, being present to the beating of my heart and softening instead of analyzing, dissecting, asking why, blaming, or being harsh.

"Today I'm going to believe that this very moment is here to awaken me, open my heart, and draw me closer to you.

"Today I'm going to believe that opening my heart feels a lot better than closing myself off, and that the holy is right here within me as I treat everyone (myself included) with a gentle regard – slow kisses goodbye, kind eyes, and gentle words.

"Today I'm going to believe that this messy, fleshy, human experience with all its brokenness and uncertainty is where your Grace shows up and miracles happen. And my job is to surrender.

"Today I'm going to believe in do-overs and beginning again.

"Today I'm going to believe that wherever I am, Love is also – alongside me, accompanying me, gently whispering prayers to my heart – to soften, to go with ease, and to love."

Prayer: God, today I have hope in my soul and in my step. I feel a surge of empowerment. I have a choice about how I want to live this day. I'm going to believe that you are right alongside me. I'm going to believe that the messy and imperfect are holy because they are sacred opportunities to hear you calling me to laugh, let go, give myself (and others) a break, and let Grace in.

Invitation: Write your own "Today I am going to believe" statement.

Doing Less

Free

Slowly, quietly,
from the deep still waters of wordless prayer
the next right step arises and I know what I must do.
My essence is no longer tethered to fear.
Softening, breathing, opening,
I am free.

Reflection

There is a beautiful Taoist adage that I have carried with me over the last several years of being a parent:

"When in doubt, do less."

I have found that when I do less – when I come into stillness, when I've done enough asking for advice or trying to figure things out – a deep peace arises. Not at first. And not "forever." But as I surrender to the "deep still waters of wordless prayer," a true knowing begins to arise and a peace settles in my nervous system. I see how my anxieties, habitual patterns, and fears begin to dissolve when I stop. Stop trying. Stop running. Stop searching. Stop talking. And as I learn how to be in Silence, Grace has room to enter.

People often ask me really specific questions related to parenting, healing our old wounds, and improving our relationships. We can talk about techniques. We can talk about solutions. But really, the answer arises by cultivating a deep regard for returning home to your own heart and being in the quiet spaciousness of the heart.

Yet we live in a culture of quick fixes and easy solutions that only address the symptoms. Being constantly "on the go," our attention is drawn outward instead of inward into our own hearts. We live in a culture of constantly searching, striving, reaching, and looking for answers. We often eat too much and work too hard in order to avoid feeling what we are feeling. We dismiss the wisdom of the sages through the centuries because it feels too hard, too raw, and too real.

Sometimes we need a guide, a companion. We need someone who is resourced and can hold space for us to turn to our own heart. We don't need *more* to do. We already "do" so much! We don't need to figure it out in our heads. We need sacred spaces that are about *un*doing. We need to create the breathing room that allows major shifts to happen, to bear witness to them, and to feel the right answers and actions arise *on their own* without harsh efforting.

This is living with ease. *This* is what I want for all of us and the whole world!

The simplicity of the wisdom in "when in doubt, do less" is often overlooked. Yet we are free in this moment to come into the quietness of our hearts, to touch beneath those surface waves to the deeper still waters, and to listen for the truth within us which whispers our next right action. Through the wordless practice of abiding with the waves of sensations and our willingness to sit and stay, a deep knowing comes into our consciousness. As we soften and breathe, we know our truth and we know that we are no longer tethered to fear. We are rooted in our truth and we touch what it is like to be free.

Prayer: God, help me to create the sacred space necessary to hear my Heart and allow my "next right action" to be revealed on its own. Please place people in my life who can hold space for me and I for them.

Invitation: When you are stressed, searching for answers, or wondering what to do, try doing less. Try asking someone to create sacred space with you to hear the wisdom of your Heart.

The Invitation

There is a sacred moment
right now
when you awaken,
you open your eyes,
and you can answer "yes" to
the invitation of your soul
to freely be who you are,
as you are,
standing or dancing
in your power.
Because today,
today, you are honoring
your truest self.
You are answering the call to
live and speak and love
as your soul speaks to you.
And this is freedom.

I Talk, God Listens

Me: "I hear you calling to me. I feel the invitation to aliveness and inner vibrancy. It used to be a soft whisper. Now it is getting louder. But I feel stuck. I don't feel like I am standing in my power. I'm not going about the day in a way that honors my truest self. This culture of parenting doesn't agree with me at all. I connect with people more on social media than in person. I eat when I'm anxious. I hurry from one thing to the next. Everyone is rushing. No one really listens deeply because they are in a hurry, holding too much, and feeling stuck just like me.

"And yet, I get it: in this very moment when I wake, I can pause and feel you calling me to live in a way that honors my soul, following your voice within me – not the voice of the world. You want me to say 'yes' to *my* soul. You promise me that in doing so in each little moment, I begin to embody a deeper sense of ease, aliveness, and inner vibrancy. This is our birthright! And my God, how far we are from it! We are stressed out, burned out, numbed out, and in desperate need of a time out. We are under resourced and overwhelmed. Every day! Enough. Enough playing the victim, enough asking someone else to rescue me with some great solution, and enough blaming the world for me feeling this way.

"My freedom lies in waking to this moment and answering 'yes' to the call of my soul to live, speak, parent, work, and love as *you* desire. *This* is freedom."

Prayer: God, I long to make contact with an inner sense of vibrancy. Keep inviting me to go about my day in a way that honors my soul's voice.

Invitation: Ask yourself, "What would it look like if I started the day in a way that honors my truest self? What if I went the whole day like this?" See an image of yourself. Then go and live it this week. Embody it.

Birthing

Something new is emerging
and wanting to be birthed.
It has wanted and waited patiently
to be in the light for so long now.
No longer okay with lying dormant,
it is ready *now*.
I *know* labor –
the waves of contractions
trembling me, moaning me
into this very moment –
where it is impossible to cling to the past
or reach for the future.
There is only "right here"
in the shaking and the trembling,
the resting and the quiet,
where even the earth echoes
the pains of labor, believing
surely I will die
yet mind, body, spirit
fully alive, present,
together breathing
the same prayer.

Death and birth meet.
No returning,
nowhere to escape,
nowhere but
here.
Somehow an ancient knowing
carries me through the waves
as I feel this painful now
and the holy unknown.
And I know with certainty
there is no going back.
Birth is happening.
As much as I want
to cling to what is familiar
I know I cannot.
There is only allowing,
opening and surrendering now.
This is how labor is.
Now something new is emerging
and wanting to be birthed.
It has wanted and waited patiently
to be in the light.
My heart is panting, pushing
to breathe the air
outside the womb.

God Talks, I Listen

God: "My Love, *you* are being birthed! You have felt the waves of contractions – the frustration, the anger, the work, the trying, and the desire to give up. There has been struggle and pushing. And now, you feel like surrendering. You are here in this very moment. It is painful. It is confusing. Doubt weighs you down, constricts your throat, and makes you want to run away. Yet birth is happening. Not even doubt or ego can stop you now. There is no going back. Give into the wisdom of your body. Roar as you need to! Cry out as you need to! Let your body make the sounds that a wild animal makes when in labor and move your body how it needs to move. *You* are being birthed, My Love. And you will soon feel the power of your lungs breathing the air outside the womb. You are being birthed. And I am here. I am here to hold you and welcome you into this new life."

Prayer: I have felt the labor pains of my own birth. I have struggled because I want control and that has made the pain more intense. I surrender. I trust that you and my soul deeply know the birthing process.

Invitation: Ask your heart, "What is wanting to be birthed – to come into form?" Create space to listen, trust, and honor the birthing process.

Noticing Signs

Journal Entry

Yesterday, our dear friend Jennifer passed away. We had all been with her the last few days at her bedside in hospice. We sang, prayed, cried, and comforted one another.

At 2 a.m. yesterday morning, I woke up and "heard" Jennifer whisper to me, *"Lis, when you get up, go outside into the field behind your house."*

Her voice was as clear as if she were in my room and speaking to me in the quiet of the night. I heard her loud and clear.

I didn't know why she wanted me to go to the field. But I was going to do it. I took Sherlock, our dog, and we went outside.

"Okay, I'm here," I said out loud, now feeling a bit foolish and wondering if my mind was playing tricks on me. It had been an emotionally difficult week, filled with both Grace and sorrow. Maybe I was making this all up in my head.

"Am I supposed to look for something?" I asked. I heard nothing.

Then I remembered Jennifer said something about sitting on a bench. I walked over to the only bench at the park. Just as I sat down, I heard Jennifer's voice, *"Look up."*

At that moment, I looked up to the patch of sky that is "my patch of sky." I look at it every morning several times – first from my bathroom window and then from our kitchen as I open the curtains for the day. I had already intentionally looked at this patch of sky several times, even while walking in the field.

But when I looked up this time, my patch of sky was completely transformed. Two planes had made a cross in the sky. In our ten years of living in this house, I had never seen that. Yes, I know, planes do this. But in that very moment?! Then, just as I saw the cross, clouds moved through, wiping it away. I heard Jennifer's voice, *"Lisa, you were with me in one of my darkest moments – my 'on the cross' moment. And now all that suffering I felt is completely gone! The Divine can and wants to wipe away all your suffering – IN THIS LIFETIME!"*

And that was it. I didn't hear her voice again. The cross was now gone. All I saw was clear, blue, open sky.

I stood there with Sherlock in the early morning sunlight, in the field, looking at the sky. Speechless. What do you do when you hear your recently deceased friend's voice and you see something you should try to rationally explain away, but you knew it had actually happened?

It felt like Easter Sunday. I was standing on holy ground – right in the field behind my own house.

Jennifer and her mom had always noticed signs: signs from the Divine – guiding, supporting, inspiring, and showing love. This was a sign. And now I'm a believer, too.

Signs of what?

Hope. Resurrection. Death does not have the final word. Love is really all there is. We have a choice: to let God wipe away all the suffering *now* – in this lifetime – and not wait until our last breath to put down the heavy bag of suffering we shoulder, and let God love us.

Prayer: God, I'm opening my eyes and heart to see signs that you are alongside me, guiding me.

Invitation: Look for signs of hope in your everyday life.

Everyday Resurrection

There comes a moment
when you know
that you can no longer keep digging in the past
searching for the magical golden "why"
that you think will finally heal
that one
tender
wound.
There comes a defining moment
when you are standing in the rain
outside your front door
with grocery bags in your hands
hungry, tired, soaking wet
and you see how all these years
you've just been running,
even if it's to therapy
you have been running
and you know
that no amount of analyzing it
is going to get you any closer
to being happy
and folding into the arms
that want to hold you
when you open that door.

The small, still voice
within you
just knows,
has known,
has been whispering to you
late at night for so long:
"There is another way, Love."
But it is finally today
that you hear her
clear and certain
as the voice
of your true God.
And you know now
there is no going back.
No talking, judging,
trying to fix it, wishing it away.
You are done
wrapping your whole self-concept
around that wound,
done believing that
there even is a wound to heal.
You stand there
soaking wet
softening
breathing
softening
breathing
opening up to
the spacious grace of emptiness
now swimming in your chest

with no desire to run and quickly fill it.
You know now what you have to do
when you open that door.
And you softly smile.

Journal Entry

I no longer believe that resurrection is only the big moment that happens after we die. It's an everyday thing. Yes, everyday resurrection. Everyday waking up. Everyday connecting to what is birthing and dying within me. Everyday giving myself permission to take the time and make the space for listening to what is birthing, what is dying, and how I am called to be with it all.

In these moments, I notice I have been holding on to old stories. I see the suffering this clinging has caused. I see the effort – the scrounging, panting, searching – that has exhausted me. And I just surrender. I let go. My grip around my stories loosens and my hands are now empty. And I am open. There is no clinging, gripping, trying, or forcing. There is just emptiness.

And that's when I am born anew. That is when God births me into a new creation! That is resurrection! I still have the scars, I still have the memories, but everything is different. And I see how I am Light, I am holy, and I am whole... and anything that tells me otherwise is a total lie.

I see how resurrection organically arises from that "spacious grace of emptiness" – the space between something dying and something new emerging. We can learn to be in that quiet, empty, holy space, filled with Sacred Nothingness where there is no looking back in sorrow at what has died and no reaching for what may be birthed. This is the space of just being and surrendering into the Grace that flows into me, breathing new life into my heart, my steps, and my loving. This is resurrection in everyday life.

Prayer: God, you call me to resurrections in everyday life. With birth comes death. In order to birth into a new creation, the old must die. Help me to be in the "spacious grace of emptiness" between death and birth. Help me to see the everyday resurrections.

Invitation: Take time to notice what is dying and what is birthing within you. Ask yourself, "How am I called to be in the spacious grace of emptiness, the space between death and birth?"

Sharing in Vulnerability

Reflection

Most of the time, it's just downright hard for moms to be vulnerable. It's hard to show your imperfections and let others in on the "secret" that you are not perfect. It can be scary to let others see that your thinking is all over the place, that you feel neurotic at times, and yes, you, too, feel alone and insecure.

It's hard because most of the time we are living in our own little worlds, going about our day with few experiences of true connection to others. It's hard for moms to be vulnerable because we're in our minivan, doing the grocery shopping between drop-off and pick-up, working, scheduling doctor appointments, and picking up new soccer cleats. It's hard because we are doing it on our own.

We can start to think, "Is there something wrong with me that I get so agitated and reactive?!" We can start to turn on ourselves.

But then you sit and have coffee with a friend, a date that maybe took a whole month to plan. You sit with that friend who really is about you, who looks at you and sees your goodness – even when your hair is a mess, even when you share a story of something you aren't proud of but is real and raw, even when you are angry, and even when you are insecure. That friend whom you can ask, "Can you help me figure this out?" Whether it has to do with your relationships, work, children, or dreams, she gets you and supports you.

It takes less than an hour to feel heard, to be seen, and to feel regarded and refreshed to go "back out there" and be in the world.

I had that kind of coffee date today.

So often in my work, I am used to being the one doing the holding – the one doing the regarding and the "holding space." I've noticed how it has grown hard for me to share, to be vulnerable, and to ask for someone to "see me" and hear me out. But every time I go into my vulnerability, acknowledge it's there, and choose to open, I am met with such compassion.

It reminds me that we have to *keep being vulnerable. Keep allowing someone in. Keep reaching out. Keep asking for someone to just "be alongside us"* in our everyday lives.

Every mom needs spaces where she can be vulnerable, imperfect, and not all together without being judged. But this takes slowing down, seeing our fellow moms, and listening for the needs – spoken and unspoken.

Being truly seen is a rare treasure in this culture of hurry. We are all so busy. Well, I don't want to be so busy that I don't see my dear friends. I don't want to be so isolated in my own world that I do not ask "to be seen."

There is an epidemic of loneliness. But I continue to be on a mission to cultivate and nourish community. And often it's just with one look of regard as we pick up our kiddos from school, inviting a friend to "hear you out," and making time to be with each other.

Together, let's just assume that at times every mom wonders if she is a good mom, she feels like she doesn't have it all together, she feels scared to show how alone or lost she is, and she could use a good cup of coffee with a soulful friend like you.

Prayer: God, you know the loneliness within me. This has made me rely solely on myself rather than reaching out for the hand of a good friend. Give me the courage to be vulnerable and connect with a good friend.

Invitation: Think of someone you know whom you'd love to be around and get to know better. Call her up. Make the effort to sit and meet her face-to-face, just the two of you without your children. Create the spaciousness to linger and be present, if only for half an hour. It's nourishing and fills your cup! Let her know that bravery isn't about being fearless; it's about being vulnerable and showing up just as she is.

Modern-day Meeting at the Well

Reflection

It was a cold spring day. I passed a mother and her child near the hot foods bar while grocery shopping. I noticed how kind she was with her curious son. I knew she had groceries to get and a plan in mind, yet she allowed space for her son's curiosity and playfulness as she shopped. There was a flow between them – a seamless synergy.

I saw them again on their way out as she paused to help her son put on his hat and mittens. She gently took her time with her squirmy and probably now hungry and tired child. I could tell she was reaching her threshold of patience.

I thought about what it takes to be grounded and resourced as a mother to respond with kindness and spaciousness. I thought about the focus it takes to maintain clarity about what truly matters. I thought about the competing forces and pressures in a woman's life and how we often feel isolated, believing it's all up to us to remain calm, energized, and in control. I see how our modern culture keeps us busy judging ourselves and thinking we have to "pull ourselves up by our bootstraps."

We aren't meant to do this alone. No other time in history have women "done motherhood" so alone! There is a deep sense of individual and collective empowerment when we believe in community and accompany each other. When we visit the communal well of togetherness, we embody our feminine strength.

We often need other women to say, "I hear you, sister," and, "I feel that, too," and, "it's not you, it's our messed up culture," and, "I'm in this with you."

I walked out of the store with this woman. I told her what a lovely presence she had and how watching her with her child was so moving. In parting, I felt as though we were two women who met at the "modern-day well" and we were going back to our daily lives richer, standing taller, and fully embodying our feminine form.

I hear the toxic messages that women receive from our culture and from growing up. I see these messages show up in my clients' bodies – the heaviness of shoulders, the tightness in the chest, and the anxiety in the belly. I see how healing it can be to walk alongside another human being. I see the aliveness that's possible through gentle and communal attention.

This is women breaking bread together. This is communion. And something deep in us remembers and longs for such communion, such meeting at the well. This is a feminine way of restoring wholeness – coming together, deeply seeing each other, acknowledging the challenges and strengths within ourselves, and empowering each other to honor our true voices.

This is the gentler, powerful work, presence, and aliveness I hope to bring to my communities. This is the modern-day "meeting at the well" and "breaking bread" that we need in our everyday lives.

Prayer: God, I need other women in my life who want to "meet at the well" and support each other. Show me who to meet this week.

Invitation: Consider creating a small group of soul sisters who want to commit to coming together on a regular basis to nourish each other.

When Others See Us

Reflection

I sat there staring at the screen on my phone. My husband was helping me make a three-minute Yoga Break video for work at the University. Three minutes turned into two hours of re-dos because I sat there watching take after take, silently critiquing the way I moved my head, wondering if my voice was too gentle, wondering if I'd put people to sleep, and critiquing every inch of myself. I started thinking, *I'm so...*

And then out of the blue, my husband said, "Beautiful." He looked up at me, having no idea the war that had been raging inside my head. "Lisa, you are beautiful."

Here I was, for hours, pointing out my imperfections, while he had been watching me – deeply admiring me. The same man who has seen me in big t-shirts and pajamas. Yelling, frustrated, and at wit's end. In vulnerable moments, struggling for 32 hours in labor and feeling like a failure. Through bad hair days, feeling insecure, and totally at a loss. He has seen me at my worst. And still, he says I am breath-taking.

That's when I "saw" myself.

I saw me as a young girl – my athletic body, insecure thoughts, passionate heart, tenacious spirit, always achieving and learning, and yet always being a poet and deeply connected to something bigger than myself.

I saw me in Latin America – where my heart was broken open by love and poverty and where I walked with the Divine so effortlessly.

I saw me dating and marrying my husband – filled with delight and a deep sense of "returning Home."

I saw me in labor and nursing my children – my changed and tired body, stressed out, alone, struggling, and then finding my groove as a parent.

I saw me now – growing into the woman I have envisioned myself to be.

I saw me in the future – an old woman, sensual, spiritual, and deeply content, with long, flowing gray hair, clear eyes, a gentle smile, and embodying softness, compassion, and delight.

In that moment I saw "me" through my husband's eyes and his overflowing, deep admiring love for me. And I saw myself as beautiful. I saw myself becoming my poetry, embodying the poems I have written and those that are still writing me.

This is the power of being seen over the years in everyday ways. First my parents "saw" me. Now my husband sees me. They have given me the eyes to see my own beauty. Sometimes we need others to reflect our goodness and beauty in order to see it for ourselves.

Sometimes we need others to keep reminding us of our goodness in order to believe it deep in our bones.

I see now how we *all* have this power.

We have the power to help our dear ones recognize their own beauty.

- ~ Our eyes have the power to mirror our children's goodness.
- ~ Our presence has the power to say, "You matter."
- ~ Our words have the power to heal deep wounds between family and old friends.
- ~ Our embrace has the power to communicate to a soul sister, "You are not alone."
- ~ Our tone of voice has the power to encourage, uplift, and inspire other people's children.
- ~ Our everyday pauses with the people we love have the power to weave a thread of tenderness and gentleness into the fabric of who our children, aging parents, partners, sisters, and brothers are.
- ~ Our touch has the power to quietly, sweetly, and tenderly reconnect with our beloved.

But our everyday "perfectly imperfect" love and presence have the power to speak what all of us – young and old – long to hear: "I see you and you are beautiful."

And we have the power to risk vulnerability, and ask one of our dear ones, "What do you see? Please tell me. I need to see my beauty and goodness."

Prayer: Divine Spirit, flow through me so I can see myself through the eyes of my beloved. Flow through me so I have the eyes to see others and remind them of their beauty. May my eyes mirror my children's goodness. May my presence say, "You matter." May my embrace be a warm blanket that communicates, "You are not alone." May my tone of voice encourage, uplift, and inspire.

Invitation: Reflect on who truly "sees" you. Notice how they see the beauty in you. What would it be like to take some time and see yourself through their eyes?

Reflect on who you truly see. Who might need you to look at them and remind them of how deeply they are loved, how beautiful they are, and how much they are regarded?

The Call to Embodied Freedom

You can slow down, My Love.
You don't have to hurry,
grasping to prove you are enough.
Massage your tight jaw.
Feel your hands caressing the tension
in your belly.
Feel your hips – your powerful, feminine
hips that know how to sway and move
in rhythmic circles dancing your
prayers.
Witness what arises –
the subtle sensations,
the waves of thoughts,
the currents of emotions.
With your hands, heart, and hips,
root into the earth
and open to the vastness of the sky
as the Beloved Within
calls you to
freedom.

God Talks, I Listen

God: "Pause and tune out the noise and distractions of the world, My Love. Feel your feet on the ground and your heart lifting up to the sky. Drop into the subtle sensations of your body. Feel the aliveness that is here right now within you. You don't have to do anything. Just feel and move with the gentle invitation of your body's impulses to sway, move, growl, pant, breathe, stomp, or sigh. Watch the currents of delight, grief, hope, and disappointment, giving them space to move through you. This is how I, as the Beloved, call you to freedom. The body is your portal to such freedom. Learn to drop into it and trust its subtle yet powerful wisdom."

Prayer: God, slowly I am learning to trust the wisdom of my body. I see my body now as a portal to you.

Invitation: When you are alone, try pausing and dropping into the subtle impulses of the body to move and make sounds. See what arises and allow it with regard and compassion.

It's Time Now

It's time now to believe
that you are good and whole,
perfect
just
as
you
are.
Yes, that's right –
exactly as you are.
Not only when you have patience,
you are Zen calm,
and you have it all together.
But also when emotions run high,
you are a mess,
and so very nervous and scattered.
It's time now to stand in your radiant beauty
exactly as you are.
Not when you lose 10 pounds,
you have a fabulous hair day,
everyone buys the novel you wrote,
and the world announces, "You've made it!"
But also when there are bulges on your sides
and your hair is a mess,
when you get yet another rejection letter
and you seriously doubt if your dream will
ever become a reality.

It's time now to know deep in your bones
that you need to be here
and that you matter.
Regardless of the story of your birth or early years,
the messages that got lodged deep inside
that you spent a fortune trying to heal in therapy.
Because you are done now
with all those doubts and stories,
beliefs and voices in your head.
You want all that energy back.
Focused.
Clear.
Potent.
Ready to be free
and do the work
you were born to do in this world.
Your innate perfection and beauty,
wisdom and radiance
are right here,
and have been here.
It's time
you embrace and embody
your inner goodness
and heal this world
with your light
and presence.
It's time now.

God Talks, I Listen

God: "Dear Heart, you have this one beautiful, glorious life to live! Enough wasting it with believing that you are not good and you are not enough! You are perfect, My Dear, just as you are! I love you whenever and however you are. The world has me all wrong! I don't desire perfection. I long for you to embrace and embody your inner goodness, to see the magnificence of your Light, to feel free, and to do what only you were born to do in this world! It's time now. I am behind you, beside you, within you, and around you. I go before you."

Prayer: It's time now, God. I hear you calling me to life. I am enough. Please keep telling me that again and again.

Invitation: Read the poem again. Choose the word, phrase, or line that resonates with you. Write it down and post it somewhere you'll see it everyday.

One Glorious First Step

There comes a time in your life when
you have to finally follow that One Desire
that has been here, inside your heart, your bones,
the very fiber of your being, for possibly decades.
Before you do anything else or put energy into
a new project or pursuit or distraction,
you must finally see and tend to this longing
that has been calling to you.

There comes a time when
you must finally have the courage
to name that
One
Holy
Desire
and gather those around you
who can hold space for you
and hear you speak this desire
into the world.

There comes a time when
you can let the tears flow now
because you are finally aligned with your truth
and in speaking it, you didn't die –
as ego and fear had you thinking for so long –

but rather now you feel a new sense of freedom
and breathing space across your chest and belly.
You embody a new sense of aliveness –
an aliveness you know as your birthright.

There comes a time when
the voices of the world begin to fade into nothingness
and you laugh now because
not even the ghost of doubt can shake you.
Instead, now what wakes you in the middle of the night
is the call of your Heart leading you
to take that one glorious first step
in the direction of Home.

Reflection

That Desire – that one Holy Desire – within you. It calls
to you. It has been whispering to you. It has grown louder
and louder. It won't be ignored. You hear it calling to you,
possibly now pounding from the insides of your ribs. You
know it. You intuitively know it is here for your own
evolution, for your family, and for the world. You know it
is like the Great Mother calling to you – calling you Home.
And yet, it frightens you. It's wild. And this wildness goes
against the ways you have been molded, shaped, and
socialized by our culture. You have spent years being
"proper" and "getting along nicely with others." And yet
late at night, this One Desire calls your name.

You may have tried to medicate it, exercise it away, shove it down with food or alcohol, or distract it with keeping your life busy. But *it will not go away.*

You feel the volcano erupting. You find yourself "losing it." There is a struggle within you. There are decades of stories and habitual ways of trying to ignore or keep down the Truth within you because you have been taught to fear the wildness of the Sacred Numinous Invitation.

Then one day – whether it is because you have hit rock bottom or you just can't take it anymore – you feel this wild courage building up within you. With every bone in your body, you know you must surrender to your One Desire. Hallelujah! And you finally turn toward this One Truth and decide to look it in the eye and say, "I am here. Take me. I surrender."

You are ready to take that one glorious first step into the seemingly unknown. Though your legs are shaking, your heart is beating a strong, powerful, certain "yes." You position your feet in the direction of Home. From behind you, the voices that once distracted, questioned, and kept you confined and shackled, now try their last attempt to call out to you. But you no longer hear them. "Not even the ghost of doubt" can taunt you or stop you.

And step by glorious step, you walk, leap, run, or dance into the arms of your One Holy Desire. You know you are Home. The wildness is freeing, liberating. You breathe how your body has known it can breathe – fully, with capacity to howl. You are alive and yet deeply grounded.

Prayer: God, with every fiber of my being, I want to let go of anything that holds me back from answering the call to take one glorious step toward embodying and living my Truth. You are the wild, numinous One I know as Home. Please help me to take one glorious step toward you.

Invitation: Create the space to listen to the One Holy Desire within you. Turn your loving gaze toward it and say, "Yes. I'm taking one glorious step toward honoring you."

Summer

The Invitation of Summer

Here

The holy is right here
in this moment.

Linger here
watching your daughter's eyelashes flutter
as she pulls you closer
in her fairy dress and pearls,
cups her little hands so softly
around your ear,
and whispers a magical secret.

Linger here
watching your son's eyes light up,
talking with his hands,
wondering how they got so big,
listening to spy tales and adventures
he has in store,
asking you to fasten all the gadgets
around his tiny waist so he can run.

Linger here
forgiving your husband
when you are angry and so very right,
taking your beloved's hand
and choosing instead
to soften and let go.

Linger here
memorizing the way he still looks at you,
wanting to make love to you,
wanting to make you happy,
wanting you to know how he sees you
embodying your power as you age,
fuller, rounder, sensual, beautiful.

Linger here
watching your children walk away from you
into class for the first time,
shrugging their shoulders,
taking it all in,
looking at you,
looking back to their class,
and finding themselves, their place,
and your years of loving them.

Linger here
noticing how your dad still calls you his little girl,
now softer, now hugging longer,
now moving slower.

Linger here
seeing how all these years
your mom just wanted you to be happy –
silently, prayerfully, gladly sacrificing her life
for yours.

Linger here
feeling your bare feet in the cool grass,
the hint of fall's arrival soon,
being breathed,
being blessed,
believing that every scar, every giggle,
every heartache, every long embrace
in this messy, imperfect, human form
is precious,
all for you to have
and let go.

Linger here
in this fleeting,
fragile, miraculous moment –
holy
just as it is.

Summer is a time of play, joy, and delight. It is about being outside, basking in the sun, and going on adventures. It can be a time of reconnecting with our dear ones and allowing a sense of ease and joy to flow in our relationships. It is a season of abundance. It reminds us to play, "linger here," and connect. We are encouraged to stop trying to *find* happiness, and instead discover it is already present. "Linger here" invites us to see how our lives are full of everyday miracles, if only we open our eyes and hearts. The delights of summer can show us that we don't have to do anything. We can just keep opening, softening, connecting, and returning "Home" to this present moment. In doing so, we discover that everything is holy.

Summer can also be stressful. As our children are out of school, we must adjust to new schedules and activities. Vacations can get hectic as well. These "summertime stressors" call for pausing, slowing down, and focusing on what really matters. Summer calls us to ask, "Is this a big deal?!"

As the heat rises, so can the "heat within us." On one hand, summer heat can bring out our sensuality. Such fire within us wants expression. And at some point in a woman's life, she finds that connecting to her sensuality and embodying its expression is liberating and exhilarating.

On the other hand, summer heat can bring out our frustration, anger, and even rage. Often we are afraid of these unpleasant feelings, so we try to push them down or get rid of them. Yet this inner heat is sacred. It needs expression and embodiment in a safe, nourishing space. We honor this sacred heat within us through connection.

These summer entries invite us to dance with this heat, remember to play, and to "linger here." They remind us to welcome both the pleasant and unpleasant as opportunities for our soul's evolution. May these summer entries connect you with your inner sensuality, support you in expressing the heat within you, and encourage you to "linger here" in the gems of your daily life.

Stay and Soften

Reflection

Many nights, I savor the moments right before bed, lying with our children. My husband often lays with our son while I lay with our daughter. Most nights I linger with her. I whisper my prayers. I lay there in the quiet, holding her and listening to her breathe.

But there are times like tonight when I think, *Oh my goodness, you have to go to sleep!* I am tired and need space. Tonight I thought my daughter was asleep as I slowly rolled out of bed.

"Mommy, where you going?" she asked.

I could've lost it. I was tired. It was late. But I remembered my practice. I felt my feet on the earth as I softened and breathed. *It's okay to feel this way, Lisa, I said to myself. It's okay to want time alone and need space.*

Then I heard, *"Mama, you stay with me?"*

STAY WITH ME. I turned back into the room, got into bed again with her, and said, *"Yes, my dear, I'll stay with* *you."* We laid like that for a long time as I softened and let go. Her words washed over me: Stay with me.

And then half asleep, my daughter whispered, *"Mommy?"*

I responded, *"Yes, love?"*

She said, *"I love you."* Then she fell sound asleep.

As I pulled the covers up over her little chest, her words were still with me: Stay with me.

Stay and soften. What if we treated every single part of ourselves with such regard? When tough things arise, what if we just "stay and soften" instead of getting more rigid or harsh?

What if we practiced this with ourselves and in our relationships with others? Just stay with what is arising. Stay with what is happening within us. And soften. Soften all our tightly wound ways of being right and judging. Soften the "perfection" mind and the "should" mind.

We tend to beat ourselves up and pile on the mom-guilt, saying things like:

"Oh, I shouldn't feel this way!" "I should be present *and* loving every minute of it." "Why don't I feel that way? What's wrong with ME?" "So-and-so would never feel like this! She loves everything about being a mom."

Instead we can practice "stay and soften." We pause. We stay with what is arising within us without judgment. We hold our hearts, needs, and yearnings close, with breath and spaciousness. We soften.

In doing so, the once intense emotions and thoughts begin to shift. What rises up is a sense of *"I'm okay. It's all okay."*

"Stay and soften" – with our own hearts, our dear ones, and with one another.

How radically different our days would be if "stay and soften" was our mantra. How much more would we be able to respond with compassion in our moment-to-moment experiences?

Tonight, I stayed with my daughter *and* I stayed with what was arising within me. I knew I needed some alone time, too. So instead of numbing out on social media, I went into my bedroom, wrote in my journal, and went to bed.

Stay and soften. This practice of tending to, allowing, and being gentle in our everyday lives can radically influence how we parent. It resources us. It creates spaciousness. And the more we offer ourselves such sweet spaciousness, the more we are able to extend that to our dear ones.

Prayer: God, show me how to 'stay and soften' when my impulse is to become rigid or harsh.

Invitation: Practice "stay and soften" the next time you get triggered.

Regard

Reflection

It was 10:30 PM in the Atlanta airport. We were coming home from ten days in Costa Rica. Our travel had started early and involved hours of driving through potholes, tending to hungry and tired kiddos, and standing in long lines. I looked over at my husband reading to our son as we waited for a connecting flight, while I held our sleepy three-year-old daughter. He paused and listened intently with a look of regard as our son interrupted him to tell a story.

I know this look very well. My husband had looked at me this way in graduate school when we started to date. He had looked at his 96-year-old grandmother this way when he spent afternoons visiting her even with his busy schedule. He looked at the teens he worked with in youth ministry this way when they went through grief-filled times of losing classmates to suicide and car accidents. He looked at the changing leaves on the trees at Walden Pond this way when we took breaks from our rigorous schedule.

It's a look of "I am totally here."

It's a look of "I see you."

It's a look of "You matter."

Still, today, he looks at me this way. He looks at me this way when we are cleaning up after dinner and I pass him the leftovers to put into the fridge. He looks at me this way when I tell him I want his thoughts (again) on a new project I have in mind, even when it's late and he still has work to do. He looks at me this way when I am teaching and I look out into the crowd to see him.

It is a look of deep regard.

It is a look of complete presence.

It is a look of total acceptance.

My husband looks at our children this way. When he is reading to them. When they interrupt him to ask questions. When they want yet another story. When our son wants to go on a nature walk. When our daughter is dancing to made-up steps and songs in the middle of the kitchen.

Sure, he gets frustrated. He's human! But the majority of the time, he has these looks of regard. And I see that these moments have an impact.

He is teaching our children to look with deep regard at the littlest of creatures and things in nature – snails, spiders, clouds, and leaves on a tree. He is teaching them to pause, look intently, and regard all of life.

When we were walking one evening in Kauai, Hawaii, my husband noticed snails crossing the sidewalk. We all paused to watch them for over 20 minutes to make sure they didn't get trampled. When my son and I were going for a walk in our neighborhood, we came to an area where new houses were being built. My son looked at the hundreds of trees that had been cut down and were stacked high, ready to be hauled away.

In disbelief, he asked me, *"Mom, did they cut all these down for houses?!"*

"Yes," I answered him. And he started to cry. His father's teachings had allowed him to see the interconnectedness and preciousness of all forms of life.

In this fast-paced, no-time-for-loving-eye-contact world, we can forget to really "see" one another. We can forget to regard one another. We can forget that all of us want to be seen, to have someone's full attention for a moment, and to be fully accepted. We can forget that each day we are dealing with tender hearts.

These daily looks of deep regard are healing. They nourish our tender souls. When I see my husband in moments like at the Atlanta airport, I softly smile and think, *This must be the way the Divine looks at us – whole, adored, and loved completely.*

Prayer: God, help me to pause in my day to really see others.

Invitation: Practice pausing, turning your whole body toward your dear ones, giving them your full attention, and really seeing them. Notice how such regard impacts them.

Linger

Journal Entry

"Mommy, you put my hair back in a ponytail, pwees?" my little three year old asks.

I put down what I am doing and look at her lovingly. My little honey's hair grows so slowly. It's fine, wispy, and sparse. She rarely asks me to do anything with it, preferring instead the surfer-girl "tousled" look.

"Sure," I say, because this is the only thing I can say to such angelic sweetness.

I slowly brush her hair. I linger, gently running the brush and my fingers through her fine curls. I'm sitting behind her – me on the couch, her standing in front of me – and my heart is full.

How rarely I get to linger like this – looking at the back of her head so close, I say to myself. Seeing her from a new angle is breath-taking and a portal into noticing anew how precious, how beautiful, and what a gift she is.

As I brush her hair, I think of the generations of moms and daughters who have sat just like this in a morning ritual that's private and sacred. Connecting as mom and daughter, slowly, sensually, sweetly. I'm not thinking of the stress between them, but rather these quiet moments of being close, holding our dear one's sweet head in our hands, slowing down, and connecting.

Something in me knows this won't always be the case – there will be struggles between us, doors closed, and her preferring to be alone rather than with me.

But we have this sacred moment right now. We are a part of a feminine circle of moms and daughters that's as ancient as human beings.

I breathe in the smell of her. I caress her little head, noticing its shape as I gently pull back her hair into a tiny ponytail.

"Finished," I say. "You look lovely." I smile admiring the blonde and browns weaving together like wheat one last time before she turns around.

She takes her fingers and traces the new ponytail a few times, studying it, marveling in it. She looks up at me, eyes completely full of delight.

"Thank you, mommy. You my best mommy," she says.

She hugs me and then runs off to the bathroom and steps on the stool to see her new look. I'm sitting on the couch, still feeling the heat from her hug contrasted with the coolness of the air where she no longer stands in front of me.

This is how the holy shines through in a day, I think to myself. I put down what isn't important. I see the invitation to delight in the ordinary and to tenderly connect.

And just like the cool empty space where she was standing, these moments are here and then gone. But I also know that these moments endure, that they are the ones which are slowly being woven into who my daughter becomes and from which she will draw when I am gone someday.

Thich Nhat Hanh said, *"The miracle isn't walking on water. It's walking on this green earth."*

Yes, he is right.

The miracle is pausing to be present...

~ to give our presence,
~ to show up,
~ to let go of keeping our fears at bay,
~ to let go of the illusion of control,
~ to let go of the belief we have all the time in the world,
~ to delight in this green earth and the people we get to see every day,
~ to see it all as a gift and an invitation into the holy,
~ to embrace this moment and linger with whoever is asking you to really see them, with tenderness and gentleness for a moment.

Whenever we can. Whenever we wake up to see such a holy invitation. And that is enough.

Prayer: God, thank you for these holy moments. I am pausing to linger and notice the holy right here in my everyday life.

Invitation: Practice pausing to linger and notice little moments in your day of delight, compassion, beauty, and connection. Savor them. Thank the Divine for them.

The Fullness of Now

I arrive right here.
Eyes closed, palms up, face the sun.
God's hand holding me.

God Talks, I Listen

God: "Go outside and get some fresh air. Feel summer's arrival. Arrive right here in this moment. Close your eyes and lift your face to the sun. I am here in this breath. I am here in the softening and letting go. I am here to hold it all and lighten what you are carrying. I am holding you."

Prayer: Beloved God, I long to feel lighter and feel your hand holding me, supporting me.

Invitation: Go outside and be. Evoke the senses – hearing, sight, smell, taste, and touch. Connect with God's promise to hold you. Imagine how the elements of earth, water, fire, and air arrive here in this moment to "hold you."

Begin Again

Conversation

Me: "We had a rough day. The kiddos were bugging each other, my husband and I got frustrated, buttons were pushed, and old habits of reacting kicked in – all before 8:30 AM. I started to take on the familiar weight of feeling responsible for it all, saying to myself, *Why aren't they getting along? I must be doing something wrong.* I had a laundry list of ways I felt like I was inadequate and failing. What do I do?"

God: "Begin again, sweet Love. You know that the 'shame and blame' game doesn't work. The 'buck up' and 'get on with it' harsh self-talk approach doesn't work. The 'yell and threaten' approach with your kiddos doesn't work. *Begin again with compassion.*"

Me: "But in the evening, it just continued. I got triggered thinking about our upcoming summer trip. I jumped on my husband for not emotionally mirroring me. And I felt horrible."

God: "Just begin again. Begin again until it becomes second nature to pause and have compassion for yourself.

In this very moment, you get grounded, you forgive yourself, and you begin again.

"Here, practice this:

Begin again.

I feel my feet on the floor. I imagine the earth beneath me. I relax my legs and sit up to allow space for my body to breathe fully.

I relax my shoulders, jaw, and face.

I feel the crown of my head rising up to the sky.

I feel my heart lifting up to the sky.

And I breathe – first focusing on exhaling fully.

I allow whatever is rising up (that cascade of emotions, thoughts, and sensations – that desire to pull away, the blame, shame, hurt, anger, fear, sadness) to BE HERE.

I hold it all with compassion and spaciousness.

AND I BREATHE. I invite myself to soften.

I keep feeling my feet on the earth, noticing my posture, opening, allowing, and exhaling fully.

I keep giving myself compassion.

I keep connecting. Even when I want to pull away. Even when I don't want to see 'that' part of me. Even when I don't want to acknowledge that I did something which makes me feel ashamed. I keep connecting – to my body, my heart, and the spaciousness created by COMPASSION.

And as I soften, allow, and connect, I open. I feel my nervous system calming down. I am able to choose more wisely how to respond."

Me: "I'll practice again and again. Thank you. This is what I needed to hear today."

Prayer: God, I see that the foundation for creating change and shifting old habits is to reconnect and begin again. I want to look at myself and my children with regard. I want to heal the shame within me that influences my reactions. Help me to forgive myself and begin again in each new moment.

Invitation: Whether you have 15 seconds or two minutes, whether you are in the car or about to get into an argument with your partner, whether you are feeling the familiar surge of shame or find yourself reacting harshly, try the practice of "beginning again."

Love Looks

Journal Entry

This afternoon, I remembered a time a few years ago when I was talking on the phone with an old college friend, while my husband and son were at the library. We had been talking for about ten minutes when my son walked in the door. *"Mama?!"* he shouted with excitement as he looked for me, found me, and ran into my arms.

"Would you hold on a second?" I asked my friend on the telephone. *"Hi, my love!!!"* I said. Looking at our two year old, I gave him a big hug and kiss. I felt the excitement of seeing him surge through my body. Then, he ran off to help dad bring the library books inside.

I returned to the phone. *"Lisa,"* my friend said, *"that is so great how you greet him. Every kid needs that. My mom never sounded excited like you just did."*

I remembering sitting there on the phone – speechless. I remember saying something like, *"You are right, friend. Every child wants their parents to be excited to see them and full of love."*

In that moment, I vowed to myself that I would always acknowledge my children when they walked through the door, no matter what I am doing.

Tonight, I was walking upstairs with my children. They are both much older now. I wondered, *Have I loved you enough?* I thought about the ways I have been frustrated and reactive. But then I thought about what my friend said. And I can see how all these years, I have been committed to Love Looks.

Love Looks: tiny moments of pausing and seeing my beloveds with eyes of compassion. Little doses of connection. Little moments of saying, "I see you," and, "You matter." Little moments when I slow down, and acknowledge the holy in the midst of getting breakfast on the table, picking up Legos, and getting organized for another day.

My friend was right. I am good at pausing and giving my children Love Looks. While they may not remember the nutritious meals I strived to make or how organized I was, they will remember these little moments of me pausing and *seeing* them. These moments are what fill a little one's sense of self slowly, in little doses over time.

Tonight, as I got ready for bed, I paused and looked in the mirror. *Love Looks*, I thought. *I could use some Love Looks, too.* I looked at my reflection with compassion. I felt the desire to practice Love Looks with myself and see the holy right here within me, too.

Prayer: May I look at myself and my dear ones with eyes of compassion. May I pause in my day and offer Love Looks.

Invitation: Our days are busy and full. Yet you can create moments to pause and practice offering Love Looks. Try it with your dear ones and yourself.

Holding Love

How many times have I rocked you to sleep,
held you, laid next to you?
I never counted.

Yes, there have been times I've counted the minutes –
the minutes until I'd get half an hour of alone time;
the minutes until I could tend to myself,
my heart's yearnings, and my healing
in the quietness at the end of the day.
I stopped "should-ing" myself into believing
this was wrong to want.
As I mother you, I am mothering myself
and I am realizing that often,
it is the fierce love we have for our children
that teaches us how to love ourselves.

YOU, my precious little ones,
are teaching me how to "hold love."

How to hold my goodness
and let go of anything
that keeps me from believing I am enough.

How to hold what is most important
and let go of what really doesn't matter.

How to hold joy
and let go of being right.

How to hold uncertainty
and let go of asking why.

How to hold grief
and let go of denying,
pushing, or analyzing.

How to hold forgiveness
and let go of blaming.

How to hold imperfection
and let go of pretending.

How to hold frailty
and let go of being strong.

How to hold prayer
while nursing, making lunches,
healing hurt knees,
and struggling to make it to Mass.

How to hold the Divine
and let go of searching.

You are teaching me,
my precious little ones,
how to hold you,
how to hold each beautiful moment,
how to hold the world in my heart
as my beloved child,

and let go
when it is time.

Reflection

Before I gave birth to my first child, I prayed for a teacher. We had just moved to a new state and I missed my teachers in Boston. Little did I know that my greatest teachers would arrive as two little infants.

This journey of parenthood is teaching me about birthing and embracing, dying, and letting go. It takes me into deep places within myself and back out into the world in ways I never could have imagined. It returns me *right here*, traversing the inner landscape of my own heart, beginning again, folding laundry, softening, reacting, and calling on God in the middle of it all.

My heart has broken open – wider and wider with each passing year as a mom. My little teachers are teaching me how to hold love – to soak it up in my bones and also to hold them and this world as my beloveds. They are teaching me how to let go – let go of my ego, expectation, and plans. They are also teaching me how to let go of them and my own life when it is time.

More and more I see this life of mine as a journey of holding, embodying, and embracing love... and then letting go. Truly this is about surrendering again and again into the arms of the Divine. Tears well up in my eyes as I learn from my greatest little teachers who I have the privilege to live with, hold, and let go of every day.

Prayer: Divine One, my children are my greatest teachers. You knew what I needed to grow and ultimately to surrender to you. Thank you for sending me my children. I bow to the ways in which they are teaching me to hold and to let go.

Invitation: Take some time to reflect on the sacred lessons your children and the journey of motherhood are teaching you.

The Wildness Within

Give In to the Wildness

Will today be another day
that you go through the motions,
that you tend to the "have to's"
and slowly feel yourself breaking
under the "shoulds"?

Will it be another day
that you spend all this energy
trying to keep at bay
the feelings finally erupting within you –
trying to tame your body's
holy impulse
to move, run, claw, pant,
moan, or leap?

There is a wildness growing in you.

The caged animal within you is no longer asking
for your permission.
It will not be silenced.
It will not go away.
It won't "roll over and play dead"
any longer.

Eventually –
when you hit rock bottom,
or you just can't take it anymore –
you will find yourself turning toward
your inner wildness, saying,

"I am here.
Take me.
I surrender."

Yes, give into this holy wildness,
the wildness within you that might scare you,
the sounds you have longed to make
but get stuck in your throat
because they aren't pretty or refined.

Today, you are done –
so very done –
with using that polite, sweet,
high-pitched voice.

No.
The sounds your body wants to make
are more guttural and wild.
They come from deep inside the belly.
They aren't logical or rational.

These wordless sounds are your medicine.
They carry the hopes of your ancestors
now realized through your raw,
embodied expression of truth.
Truth that has been
pushing against your ribs
to be spoken out loud
for too long now.

So let it begin with one sound –
one awkward, embarrassed-at-first,
growl, sigh, or pant –
a sound that makes no sense
but speaks your untamed truth.

Alone in your car,
on a hike in the woods with a friend,
or in your kitchen with dirty dishes in
the sink and your children looking at you –

let the sound come!

Feel it rising up from your belly,
vibrating your lungs, heart, and throat.

Then listen for the next sound
and then the next, and the next,
allowing the holy waters of wildness
to burst open the doors of your caged longings
ready to be set free.

Yes.
Give in to the wildness
that will surely undo you, shake you, moan you,
and dance you as embodied prayer,

pulsing, naked, and
finally
so
very
alive.

I Talk, God Listens

Me: "There is a heat rising within me. It is a holy wildness that grows louder. I hear it in my clients. I hear it pushing against my own ribs. This heat outside calls me to honor the "heat within." It is like a volcano ready to explode. I've tried to hold back strong feelings – feelings I don't even have words for but long to be expressed, felt, embodied, and released. I'm terrified. Yet the more I try to 'keep a lid on it,' the more the anger and resentment seep out. I find myself reacting over little things. My husband looks at me like, *Where did that come from?!*

"This is where it comes from – in all of us:

- ~ Not tending to ourselves
- ~ Stuffing down our voice
- ~ Waiting for someone else to rescue us
- ~ Tending to everyone else and neglecting our needs
- ~ Taking on way too much
- ~ The pressure of perfection and 'doing it all'
- ~ Living on a daily basis in a way that doesn't really jive with our souls
- ~ Traumas we have held within us for too long now

"It's off balance. Unattended frustration turns to anger. Anger begins to turn outward in blame or inward as depression. And a rage builds within us.

"This rage is righteous. It wants to be harnessed and channeled. It wants holy expression! And yet we are a culture that tries to refine and tame our body's holy impulse to move and make the sounds that it must make – to pant, growl, cry, shake, and moan – that shake off the accumulated stress within us. So we try to tame it. But it won't be silent! It wants expression!

"Eventually, the Holy Wildness calls us to authentic expression. It is time to let the Holy Wildness move and make the sounds it has longed to make. The heat of summer invites us to let the rage rise as embodied expression in a way that is harnessed – not out of control – but rather channeled and finally allowed to breathe."

Prayer: Dear God, I feel this sense of rage building in me. I've tried to deny it and stuff it down. It doesn't work. It comes out as anger and meanness. Help me to honor this rage and give it the sacred space it needs.

Invitation: Notice the "heat within you." Start with little drops of frustration. What does frustration feel like in your body? Where do you feel it? What sound does it want to make? How does it want to move your body? Allow frustration to make the sounds and move your body – with mindfulness and compassion. Notice what sense of freedom arises within you as you give expression to frustration.

Orienting Toward Pleasure

Journal Entry

When my daughter was two, I looked in the rearview mirror of the car, and I saw her slowly and happily smoothing hummus all over her face. She was totally present to the experience and delighting in it. The look in her eyes and the smile on her face told me how much pleasure she felt in that moment. Sure, I wondered how we would get it all off without making a huge mess. But in that moment, my daughter's deep connection with sensation and pleasure was so powerful that my only response was delight. I knew I was on holy ground. My daughter was teaching me how to orient toward pleasure in the smallest of things. And I knew enough to join in her delight and support her in continuing to feel such "in-the-moment" pleasure.

I shared this memory with a colleague today and she said, "Lisa, that is beautiful." She went on to tell me how, when she was little, she had long, beautiful hair. She loved her long hair. But it often got tangled. Her mother would sit there combing out the knots while my friend would tell her mom how much it hurt. "And my mom would say to me: beauty comes with pain."

This is the early message my colleague learned about pleasure, pain, and beauty! I don't blame her mom – she grew up hearing this same message. But listening to my friend, seeing the sadness in her eyes, and hearing how this message shaped her, I resolved to be mindful of how I help shape my children's relationship to pleasure, pain, and beauty.

Pleasure is so very warped into crazy things in our culture! I want to show my children how it is to feel good in their bodies in positive ways. I want them to know delight and pleasure in the simple things of life. And I want them to know how to lovingly tend to pain when they experience it – to know they are worthy of caring for themselves and healing pain. It's such a gift to be embodied and experience being alive. And I am creating the space for them to love that aliveness.

This means I must "orient toward pleasure," too. When I go around stressed, pleasure is the first thing to go. I focus on what's wrong. I try to control things. I blame. I only see the unpleasant. This is a call for me to practice "orienting toward pleasure." This is a call for me to remember how delightful it is to be alive and experience the sensory pleasures of being embodied.

Prayer: God, you know the experiences I have had and the messages I have learned in this life about pleasure. Help me to heal any messages that no longer serve me and keep me from feeling the full aliveness of being embodied. I want to feel pleasure. I want to notice pleasure in my everyday life.

Invitation: For a period of time, devote your attention to "orienting toward pleasure." Notice what is enjoyable to you. When you experience pleasure, how is it to feel it in your body? What does it taste like? What does it smell like? What does it look like? Evoke all the senses. Notice the effects of "orienting toward pleasure" in your day.

Love Lists

Reflection

Most of us don't start out marriages being cranky, controlling, and blaming. Throw in stressful mornings trying to get the kiddos to school, middle-of-the-night stomach viruses, changing jobs, losing jobs, a health scare, or the death of a loved one and we can be stressed out. Our relationship with our beloved goes by the wayside.

With little time to reconnect or reconcile, we can we lose a month, a year, or even a lifetime to our "default stress mode" instead of our "I love you" mode.

I've seen it in my own self and the women I work with every day. It happens slowly over time. The daily stress and overwhelm become our daily habit. We can start to point out the negative in our husbands – a lot. We can start to blame and turn away from them. We can become bitter, cranky, and controlling.

It happened to me. Being pregnant was hard for me. Even though I taught yoga and saw psychotherapy clients up until week 38, I always felt sick and in pain. Throw in 32 hours of labor, a sudden C-section and nursing challenges, and things were rough.

Parenting is like that. It's so much harder than we could have ever imagined. I'm talking "soul-changing, learning to live with the unknown, seeing your heart now walk outside of you, tested to the limits and then beyond, and being completely responsible for the life of another human being" kind of hard!

Don't get me wrong – it's hands down the most incredible, life-changing, joyous thing, too.

But in the years of sleepless nights, recouping from pregnancy, finding the "right" preschool, navigating playdates, finding and embodying our parenting style, entering the school-aged season of your family, doing math homework, running from one activity to the next, and tweens becoming teenagers, we can forget to nurture our relationship with our partner.

I had an incredible position at Georgetown University. I loved it. But I found myself increasingly critical of my husband and short with my kiddos. One night we were getting ready for bed. I looked into my daughter's closet and couldn't find the pullups. The clean clothes weren't "put away right." My kiddos were jumping on top of each other.

I lost it. "Brian!" I started, "Why in the heck aren't these clothes put away? Couldn't you do it?!" I started getting into no-one-helps-me mode.

Then I heard my daughter say, "Yah, Bwwwian!"

I stepped back. I heard myself. I heard *me* in her. And that was my tipping point. I made a big change. I left my position at Georgetown and started doing consulting with them and other organizations. I made sleep a priority. I exercised more. I took back the energy I was expending on commuting and put it into being present the way I wanted to be. We cut our budget in half *and* I dedicated financial resources and time to taking care of me.

I started to appreciate my husband. I began to write Love Lists: lists of what I appreciate and love about him. I started to notice the good again. I started to share with him what I appreciated about him.

It took many years (yes, years) to shift the rut I was in. By making big changes that nourished my own well-being and making my Love Lists, slowly we began to come back together. We began to turn toward each other. Today, we still share our Love Lists. And we make *us* a priority.

Prayer: God, I could turn bitter. This tells me that I'm not nourishing myself enough. Help me to make the decisions to care for my wellbeing. Help me to speak up for myself and share my needs. Help me to have the patience to listen to my husband and what he needs. I want to turn toward him. I want to nourish our relationship. I want to notice the good.

Invitation: Make your own Love Lists. At first you may not feel like it. Yet begin to write just one or two things you appreciate about your husband every day. When you feel comfortable, share your Love Lists with him.

Make Time for Joy

Reflection

Last night, my daughter and I were outside going for an evening scooter ride. My son called to me, "Mom, I'm leaving for Scouts," as he leaped down the front stairs to jump into the car with my husband. "Wait!" I called out to them, "I'd love a hug!"

I walked toward them with my arms stretched out. And there he was – my six-year-old son in his Tiger Cubs uniform. Suddenly a wave of nostalgia swept over me.

Standing before me, my son looked older. My heart ached. I found myself wanting to hold onto my little boy. "Dear God," I quietly breathed, "this is going too fast." And yet, I knew it was impossible to stop time. I could also see the grown man in him. I could sense all the moments of us holding, letting go, hugging, sadness, laughing, and sharing joy. My heart was full and content.

I could've bowed down right there on the holy ground of the sidewalk. I knew there was an invitation in this moment and every moment ahead of us. *"Dear God,"* I found myself praying, *"let me make time for joy. Let me make time to really be here and notice the good."*

When I start to go down that path of wanting to control something like how neat their rooms are or how perfectly they write, *"Dear God, let me choose to let go and focus on what matters most and connect with them."*

When I start to get stressed out and the kiddos are making lots of noise, *"Dear God, let me choose to get grounded and soften."*

When I start to rush, *"Dear God, let me choose to slow down, exhale, connect, and even have FUN!"*

When I get bogged down in what we have to do – whether it's getting dinner on the table, getting out the door, or getting the kiddos a bath, *"Dear God, let me lighten up and choose to enter into it with JOY."*

That's my prayer for this new season. Can I take myself and my plans less seriously and have fun? Can I choose joy? I'm not talking about every single minute. I'm not going to put yet another pressure on me. But I feel the call to *make time for joy* in our everyday life.

Prayer: Dear God, help me to lighten up and choose joy in our busy schedule.

Invitation: Just today, look for one way you can choose joy. Create it. Embrace it. Savor it.

A Speck of Stardust

I'm in Mass listening to the
Prayers of the Faithful being read,
the time when we bring forth our prayers.
I'm savoring the silence, the chance to be still, when
the lector reads, "...and for all those who have died,
especially..."

And I hear a whisper from within me,
"Someday, your name will be read."

I think about the Mass soon after I have passed away.
How old will my children be?
How will they respond to hearing my name?
I'm sure there'll be people in the pews who don't bat an
eye, don't recognize the name, are bored,
and ready for Mass to end.
One Mass, one time, one little moment,
my name will be read;
the soundwave of my name travels in all directions
for a short moment until it reaches Silence,
dissipates, and new sounds arise.

Somehow this seems fine, even perfect,
and how it "should be."
I am aware now, sitting here at Mass, quiet,
next to my beloved,
how I am one grain of sand on a beach that
stretches to limitless ends,
one speck of stardust in an infinite universe.

It "rights" my thinking,
and nestles me into my place across time.

I look at my beloved.
I feel the heat of our hands touching,
I hear the cantor now singing.
Just a few generations from now, no one will exist who
remembers me in form, who felt my touch,
felt the palpable sweetness between
me and my beloved, who knew the exact way
my eyes lit up seeing my children.

It makes this moment a sacred opportunity,
this moment that I am still in form, with arms to hug,
eyes to behold, words to whisper, like
"I love you" and "please forgive me."

I have no idea what happens
when the memory of each of us fades,
as if we never existed.
But somehow, I believe that our sound
is carried in the sweet song

of our great grandchildren humming a lullaby,
our touch is felt in the gentle way
our descendants walk on this earth,
and the one speck of light we are
finds its way into the hearts of all we have beheld
and illuminates the path to Love
until we all return to Silence.

I Talk, God Listens

Me: "In Mass today, I suddenly stopped. I sensed my place in the order of things. I was sitting next to my husband when I realized that someday they'll read my name as part of the prayers for all those who have died. Maybe it's tomorrow, maybe it's 50 more years from now. But the truth is, I'll cease to exist. I get it, God.

"I sat there in the silence with the reality swirling through me that I am just a speck of stardust. And that's okay.

"In becoming a mom and bringing forth life, I have also felt Death as my constant companion. I am aware that you know the exact number of breaths we will take. From our first breath as newborns, we are one breath closer to our last one. This reality doesn't have to scare us. It can call our attention to what is most important.

"Today, God, I remembered my impermanence. I remembered my place in the order of things. And I feel you gently showing me that there are many moments where I could say, *'No big deal'* and let go of trying to control it all. There are other moments when I can wake up and say, *'This is important. Turn toward your dear one and look!'* And that one moment can change everything. It can change how I go about my day and it can change the lives of my children and their children.

"We are only one speck of stardust and yet, as the poet Rumi says, *'In your light I learn how to love.'* In my light my children learn how to love, how to hold this world with gentleness, how to see their own beauty, and how to see the light in others. And it happens in *moments*.

"So, God, I can say to the mess of Legos on the floor, *'No big deal.'* I can see the opportunity to connect with my children and say, *'This is important. Turn toward them and look!'*

"Thank you, God, for Mass today. I see how I have some light to shine. I have some noticing and looking to do."

Prayer: Beloved, more and more I sense my own impermanence. Someday, I will cease to exist. Stay close to me. Whisper reminders to me of how to live each moment and surrender to you.

Invitation: Reflect on impermanence. A beautiful practice is to ask: What if I had one year to live? Six months? A month? A week? A day? An hour? A minute? Notice what truly becomes important to you. Notice how this influences the way in which you go about your everyday life.

What Remains

I see now how this life is fleeting.
Every breath,
every time my little ones
wrap their tiny arms around my neck
and shout, "Mama!"
every gleeful plea for
"one more story" at bedtime
is holy
ripe and ready in this moment to savor,
then it is gone.

Like a breeze that flutters the curtains in my room,
kisses my skin on a warm summer night,
then returns to where it came
and only stillness remains –
I see how fleeting my life is.

Suddenly from darkness I am born,
I caress this world with my gentle presence
for only a short while,
then I return to where I came
and I am no more in this form.
What remains?

I want it to be my thousand gentle kisses on
my children's foreheads before going to school,

my slow caress on their backs they've felt
a million times as they drift off to sleep,

my voice of steadfast encouragement
at decisive moments to leap and
follow their hearts,

their inner prompting to notice suffering
and respond with compassion
as they've seen my hands
and heard my soothing words
hundreds of times on ordinary days,

the everyday moments of me returning to
my holy stillness that slowly filled them –
like sweet, sacred drops of holy water –
with an inner quiet that sustains them
when life shakes them,

the words I've whispered into their being
a million times a million times,

"You are my delight."

Reflection

As we go about our everyday lives, it can be hard to
parent with the "bigger picture in mind." We are focused

on getting out the door, making sure everyone is wearing shoes, and figuring out what in the world we'll have for dinner tonight. What do we want to remain with our children when they are grown? When they have children of their own? When we are gone?

When we answer those questions, the "now" becomes ripe with opportunity for filling our children with what we want them to remember, embody, and become many years from now. Our relationships with our children are literally wiring their brains. The tone of voice we use and how we pause, look at them, and listen are moments of feeling regarded that are woven into their being. When we caress their backs, read them a story, or go outside to play basketball with them, we are sending the message, "You matter to me." Also, we model healthy habits of self-care when we nourish ourselves with quiet moments of stillness, exercise, and rest. We show them that caring for self is caring for others. All these experiences become who they are and how they carry us with them long after we are gone.

This reality can gently empower and focus us. Living in our "go, go" culture, our stressed nervous systems react with only the short-term in mind. Parenting with the bigger picture in mind takes pausing and sitting with what we want to remain in our children many years from now and gently reminding ourselves of the answer before we respond to life's everyday challenges.

Prayer: God, more and more I am aware of our mortality. It both scares and focuses me. Help me to parent in the little moments of everyday life with this bigger picture in mind.

Invitation: Take some time and reflect on this: "What do I want to remain with my children when I am gone?" Let this "big picture" focus inform today's "in the moment" response.

Fall

The Invitation of Fall

Come Closer

What if one day
you let the sadness,
the grief stuck under your ribs,
the regret lodged in your throat,
the shame still folding down
the corners of those precious lips

to come closer,
to not push them away
or angrily shake your finger
scolding them
for their persistent presence,
and instead chose to say,

"For so long I have tried to avoid you,
ignore you, medicate you,
keep my distance from you.
But today,
today I am tired.
I am tired of the effort it takes.
Today,
please,
come closer.

Let me breathe, sit, cry, moan,
dance, and hold you.
My precious friends, yes,
I call you friends.
Because I see
there is no other way to wholeness.
There is no other practice or strategy to try.

Just this.

Arms vulnerably outstretched,
heart bursting, beating wildly,
wanting now to only draw you closer
into my arms, my chest
and ever so tenderly
let you weep,
let you fold into me
like a babe in his mother's arms,
my hand caressing you,
my sweet whispers soothing you
until our tears
begin to shine in the moonlit night,
turning into jewels
that become our offering to the Divine
who has been waiting for so long now
to hold us..."

What if today is that day?

Fall brings cooler weather and new energy. For many of us, fall can feel like the start of a new year. As school begins again, our activities and commitments begin, too. The hustle and flurry of activities can quickly consume us. Fall invites us to get focused in an intentional way.

Creating rituals in our everyday lives helps us to focus on what truly matters. Before the schedule becomes full, fall's invitation is to pause and consider what daily rituals we can bring into family life that will nourish our connection to one another.

Fall is also a season of grief. Our old griefs come to the foreground of our consciousness to be acknowledged with our compassionate attention. Yet it can be scary to pause and see our sadness and grief. We can busy ourselves as a way to avoid feeling. As the poet, Rumi, says in the poem, "Guest House," we can welcome these griefs knowing they are clearing us out for some new delight. If we gently allow these griefs to "come closer," we may find that such radical tenderness heals what we might have been afraid to feel. When we embrace such a radical posture of befriending our griefs, gratitude and forgiveness arise more spontaneously and fully.

Fall invites us to remember those parts of ourselves that we have ignored or pushed away, and instead ask, "What if today I chose to draw these parts closer? What if today I chose to practice radical gentleness with my sadness and grief?" With mindful attention and radical gentleness, we remember what integration feels like. We remember that wholeness is our birthright.

With rituals, tending to grief, forgiveness, and gratitude, we honor the invitation of fall and can welcome the holidays with a deeper sense of compassion and a buoyant sense of delight.

May these fall reflections invite you to pause, heal the griefs that arise and want your compassionate attention, and connect you with an inner sense of gratitude and delight.

Mindful Moments

Journal Entry

It's the start of a new school year. I could easily get consumed by the "to do" list and wrapped up in all that needs to be done. I could easily lose sight of what really matters and get lost in distractions. I could easily make it a habit of hurrying, hustling the kiddos, carting them from one activity to the next, and never pausing to really *see* them.

When my children were infants, I used nursing as an opportunity to have a "mindful moment" of connection between us. When they were toddlers, I used to pause when I was putting them into their car seat or getting them out of the seat. I would look into their eyes and smile before we ventured out into the world. These were tender moments of sacred connection. These "mindful moments" could easily get hurried, passed over, or ignored. But somehow, I had the wits about me to pause and see them.

These days, our schedules are full. Just getting out the door and to school on time can be a challenge. Picking them up from school, we could easily miss the opportunity to pause for a "mindful moment."

Last fall, I made a vow to myself: when we greet each other, when we say goodbye, and when we reunite, I will create "mindful moments" and they will become our sacred rituals of connection.

For the past year, this is what I have been doing:

~ in the morning when we all wake up, I pause and say, "Good morning, sweet love!" We hug and I acknowledge them. We linger and cuddle. I give them my presence.

~ before they walk into school, we pause and hug. I give them my presence and my smile. No matter how late we are. No matter how hurried the morning has been. I want the last moment before my babies head off "into the world" to be one of connection because I never really know if that'll be the last time we see each other.

~ when they come home from school, I stop what I am doing. I turn my body toward them. I give them my presence. I hug them and look them in the eyes. I linger. It will only take a few extra moments. But for those few minutes, I am totally present.

~ at bedtime my husband and I both lay with our kiddos. Yes, I am often really tired. I have been going for 14 hours. But I can lie with them in the darkness. I feel their bodies become still. I feel their breath become deeper and longer. Sometimes there are things that they bring up and talk about – in the darkness, in the stillness. And I tell myself, "This is what matters. Just be here." Yes, there are times when I am too tired and I need space for just being alone. But I've eased up on myself about that. That's okay to feel, too. I am human.

These "mindful moments" in our day are sacred rituals. They are moments of prayer. They are like the meditation bells of a monastery ringing at specific times in the day reminding us to "come back to center" and notice where our attention is. Doing this for a year, these "mindful moments" become woven into our bodily memory so we do them instinctively. And when we have had a tough day – we've been unkind or harsh with each other – we have these "mindful moments" structured into our day to help us reconnect. They are a built-in invitation to begin again.

Prayer: God, I need these "mindful moments" in my day to stop what I am doing. They are my meditation bells, my call to prayer, and my reminder that connecting to my dear ones is what matters most. Help me to create these sacred rituals and weave them into our everyday life.

Invitation: Identify a few moments in the day that you could turn into "mindful moments" where you stop what you are doing, pause, look at your dear ones, and connect. Make them your sacred rituals. See them as your meditation bells and your call to prayer.

Reclaiming the Sabbath

Conversation

Me: "It would be easy to take off running this fall and fill our schedules with activities. God, I see how everyone needs a Sabbath – a day, or even just a few hours – of total rest. Repose. Quiet. I know this, and yet when I begin to just be still and do nothing, I feel guilty or like I 'should' be doing something. But this morning, after I drop off the kiddos at school, I'm going back home and doing nothing. No checking Facebook or email. No writing or planning. Just pure repose. Quiet. I want to allow the symphony of silence to sing within me and through me for a whole morning. That's a Sabbath for a mom."

God: "I love that language: 'a symphony of silence.' Yes, Dear Heart, everyone needs a Sabbath. It might take some time to get used to 'doing nothing.' Your mind will wander. You'll feel the urge to get up and do something. But the more you build this Sabbath into your week and make it a weekly ritual, you'll settle into the silence. You'll long to hear that symphony. And you will feel renewed. So make it a habit – a weekly habit. I'll meet you there, my Dear Heart."

Prayer: God, help me to create the space in my week for a Sabbath. Whether it is for a few hours or a full day, I want to make this a weekly ritual and build it into my schedule. Please help me to do this.

Invitation: Consider blocking out just a few hours a week for a Sabbath. Do nothing. Just rest in the way that this season calls to you. But make it a weekly ritual.

Embodying Sensuality

Reflection

I welcome the change in the weather. The crisp air against my skin is refreshing and invigorating. I packed up our summer clothes and stored them in the back of the closet. I replaced the sandals for shoes. I went through the kiddos' cold weather clothes to make sure they had enough pants, long-sleeved shirts, and socks. I now look at my own wardrobe and realize it's time to go through my clothes, too.

I decide to do this myself and do what I can in two hours. I take each piece of clothing and ask myself questions. Is it a fabric that feels soft and lush against my skin? How do I feel in this? Is it comfortable? Is there anything that's too tight and I've been holding on to for several years now hoping I'd lose some around my middle? It's time to let those go. It's time to love my belly as it is – along with my hips, thighs, and breasts.

I put my hand on my belly and feel the fleshy skin of a 40-something woman having carried and birthed two babies. My hands lovingly rub my stomach. I look in the mirror – me in my bra and underwear. I have a different body now than in my twenties. I am rounder, yet still strong. I look at my breasts. These breasts have fed babies for over four years. I bring my hands to my hips and slowly begin to sway. My hips now know how to move in rhythm with my husband's body for pleasure – his and mine.

I am a sensual woman. Now I embody a sensuality that one can only learn over time through pleasure and love, surrendering and opening, receiving and becoming vulnerable. I can visually see how I am dropping into my divine feminine power as I let go of the unhealthy expression of masculine power. I feel the union of divine masculine and feminine taking root in me – fierce power rising within – like lava.

There is a pile of clothes now to donate. I don't keep anything that is restrictive or tight. The clothes that remain are ones that honor and adorn the rising of my sensual self. It feels good to have given myself two hours to go through my clothes and keep only what makes me feel beautiful and sensual as my body is right now.

Prayer: God, my body has surely changed over the years. Help me to see the beauty within me as I am. Help me to more fully connect with my sensual self.

Invitation: Consider taking time to go through your closet and keep only the clothes that make you feel beautiful when you wear them.

Radical Tenderness

God Talks, I Listen

God: "You know those 'broken' parts of you? The parts that feel lonely, angry, sad, or ashamed? Those are the parts that need the most love. My Dear Love, our world needs radical tenderness. Can you hold your disappointment, old wounds, and even hatred with the tenderness of a mother drawing her child close to her heart? The voices of the world can be so harsh. Today, can you be a voice of tenderness? Can you talk tenderly to yourself, especially the parts that feel most broken? Can you talk tenderly with your husband, your children, and your parents?"

Prayer: God, you call me to practice radical tenderness with myself and this world. Let your tenderness flow through me – in my eyes, arms, hands, feet, the pace I take, and the words I speak.

Invitation: It takes practice to be "counter cultural" and offer tenderness to the parts of us we would rather push away. Yet this is how we heal and how love grows in our children's hearts and in this world. Be a source of radical tenderness today. Start with yourself. Talk to each part of yourself with kindness and tenderness as you go about your day.

Notice the Good

God Talks, I Listen

God: "My Dear, there is so much good in your life. There is so much beauty in your day. I want you to be able to see it and to 'take in' such blessings so your shoulders relax, the tension between your eyes softens, and you reclaim the aliveness within you.

"I know what holds you back. You think that if you notice the good, we won't tend to what hurts within you. You want to be seen. Every human wants to be deeply seen. I see your tension. I see how responsible you feel. I see what you have been carrying, how hard you try, how deeply you love, and how you strive to make it right for everyone. I see all this, My Love.

"And, too, I see the loving way your husband looks at you and desires you to be happy and at ease. I see how your daughter's face lights up when you walk into the room and how she loves you just for who you are. I see how your son looks up to you and asks for your guidance. I see how your whole body softens and you breathe with such ease, My Dear, when you gently place your attention on the abundance of sweetness, beauty, and goodness in your day. Such gratitude, ease, and softness create the container to hold your sorrows. They make your heart tender, open, and expansive.

"I am here in it all. Feel my love in the way your husband's eyes adore you, your son's voice calls for you, and your daughter's arms reach for you. Feel my love in the soft way your mom always calls and says uplifting words to soothe you. Feel my love in your dad's quiet way of making sure you are cared for. Feel my love in the way you pull back the kitchen curtains in the morning, see a magnificent sunrise, and the beauty moves you to tears. Feel my love in the way the morning breeze caresses your skin as you take the puppy for a morning walk.

"Dear Heart, these are all here for you – to ease your heart, mind, and body. These are all here for you to deeply enjoy... and so you become a blessing to all those you'll greet in a day."

Prayer: God of abundant blessings and goodness, sometimes all I can do is notice the negative. Open my senses to deeply notice and take in the good. May your goodness fill me with tenderness and aliveness so I may be a blessing to those around me. I am so very grateful for these blessings.

Invitation: There are many ways to "notice the good" as you go through your day. Before you roll out of bed, pause for a moment. Do you feel the air coming into your body and your lungs expanding? You are alive and here for another day! Feel this gift. Notice the good around you: the soft covers, a warm home, hot water for your shower, or the way the sunlight filters into your bedroom. Notice the good within you as you look in the mirror. Look for the good in others as you see people in your day.

End your day with recalling all the good you experienced – an unexpected call from a friend, a kind gesture from a co-worker, the vibrancy of the sun on a cold day, the way your child said "mom" or "dad," the food you ate, and the warmth and love that surround you. This soothes the nervous system and readies you for sleep.

The Depth of Devotion

Reflection

I went outside this morning to warm up the car before taking my children to school. As I sat in the cold driver's seat looking at the ice-covered windshield, I thought about how many times my dad, during 40+ years of getting up early before any of us and going to work, must have gotten into a cold car, and if his car was in the driveway instead of the garage, how many times he must have cleared off the windshield. I thought about all those years of "doing what he had to do" to care for us – sacrifices that I know about and those that are only known to him and my mom.

I thought about my mom – a mother of four – and wondered how many times she too went out in the cold to warm up the car and take us to school. I thought about all the years she held things together, on her own, with no space to fully grieve losing her parents in her early twenties.

I thought about the French braids she would so lovingly put in my hair and I wondered how she did it – how she could sit and patiently braid my hair in the morning before school with three other children running around. I never remember feeling rushed or blamed for taking too much time or wanting too much. I remember her kindness, attention, and devotion to loving.

A deep sense of gratitude overwhelmed me as I watched the windshield wipers going back and forth. I looked up at our house. I could see our puppy watching me and wagging his tail. I could see my children putting their coats on and getting their backpacks. I found myself pausing as tears welled up in my eyes. There were many years when I couldn't see past the imperfections in others in order to have gratitude for the "depths of devotion" of my dear ones and my own self.

I thought about a few weeks ago when someone was complaining about a gift her mother-in-law had given her at Thanksgiving. I remember thinking, *Gosh, where's the gratitude? At least she was trying.* I remember then thinking about the times I've complained about my own parents "not getting it right" and how sorry I am now, as a mom myself, for nit-picking at the imperfections rather than appreciating the depth of devotion.

How often do we nit-pick at the imperfections of our dear ones – our parents, our spouse, our children, and even ourselves? How often do we hold ourselves and others to impossible standards?

I see the suffering this has caused me and my dear ones. I see, too, how I nit-picked for all these years because I was hurting. And I have needed to tend to old wounds that just happen when we are in intimate, so-very-human relationships with others. I have needed to acknowledge the unmet needs and tend to those wounds.

That has taken many years. Having children brings up our old, unresolved stuff, doesn't it?

But over the years, by tending to the old hurts I'm no longer stuck. I complain less and take responsibility for my own happiness. I recognize when I go into "victim" and "blame" mode, and ask clearly for what I need.

This has been empowering. I have softened. I have released and let go. I have more spaciousness and capacity to let others off the hook.

Most importantly, my capacity to see and appreciate my dear ones' depth of devotion has widened. Rather than stewing over old wounds from the past and nit-picking imperfections in the present, I can see the devotion – even in the human "imperfections." And my heart swells with gratitude.

I can let myself be imperfect, too. I can let myself "off the hook." I can see the depths of my devotion to my children and husband. I can see the bigger picture. I can actually pat myself on the back and say, "Lisa, you have really done all you can. You have been deeply devoted." I can forgive myself. And there is a widening sense of ease and strength settling in my soul.

When I'm working with clients in therapy or coaching and they are upset with someone and wrapped up in the details of the story, I'm listening for the need under the complaint. I lead them into a body-centered practice of learning to tend this need. I've seen this again and again

– when we pause and see what is beneath the complaints, we tend to the wounds there rather than staying stuck in nit-picking the imperfections. We begin to heal. We begin to release all that energy caught up in blaming and "turning away from love" that has robbed us of our inner vibrancy. We begin to widen the lens and see the depth of devotion – in others and ourselves. Our capacity for gratitude widens. Our ability to love and treasure ourselves and others deepens. We touch what it is like to breathe and love freely.

Prayer: God, I want to tend to the unmet need and wounds within me rather than nit-picking the imperfections of others and myself. This holiday season, help me to have eyes to look for and see the depth of devotion of my dear ones and myself.

Invitation: Over the holidays, when you catch yourself complaining about others – especially your dear ones – what would it be like to ask, *"What's the unmet need within me?"* What would it be like to tend this wound rather than continuing to nit-pick the imperfections? Can you sense your capacity widening to see their depth of devotion in the imperfect, human ways of loving?

The Grief that Won't Go Away

Beneath the hurry and worry,
beneath the frazzled scurrying for control,
beneath the frustration turned resentment,
beneath the fear that comes out as anger,
pointing out the tiny mishaps of your child or partner,
and momentary explosions over dishes left in the sink
or mud tracked in on the kitchen floor,
is grief.
Grief that has been beating against the insides of your ribs
longing to be breathed, acknowledged,
and tended to.
And she will not go away.
She will stay buried for only so long,
and then she will begin beating her drums,
rhythmically calling to you
over and over and over again.
"I am here," she will say. "See me.
I am not your enemy.
I am your gateway to freedom."
She wants you.
And you fear she will devour you.
She will.

But she will not leave you crushed and broken.
She will not leave you on your hands and knees
finally falling apart with palms beating the kitchen floor.
Oh no.
She will unravel you, for sure.
But she will not leave you.
She is holding space –
precious, embodied space –
for you to let the waves of emotions move
through your body.
The waves that must come, must be felt,
not analyzed with well-crafted words
sitting and talking in therapy.
But rather with groans and sounds
only a hurt animal knows
to be holy.
She is not afraid of those sounds.
She is not afraid of the tsunami
stuck inside of you.
She is not afraid of your body
moving and thrashing in ways
you've never allowed yourself
to move before.
She holds space for you.
She will dismantle any notion
that you are in control of this life.
And while this may drive you mad at first,
that struggle is temporary.

Because as you move and groan,
weep and cry out,
the alchemic wisdom of the body
is carrying the very medicine you need
to surrender any belief that you are alone,
that you could ever be separated
from Love.
In the spaces between breaths,
in the silence between sobs,
you feel it.
Grief has carried you
into the arms of the Beloved.
And though you still feel tender and broken,
somehow you know that death will not
have the final say.
You feel Grace quietly lying there with you
on the cold floor.
Your dog walks over to lick your face.
You feel your breath filling you again.
And you sense that Grief is no longer your enemy.
She is your companion who remembers
what is eternal.
And she will stand at the threshold
of this world and beyond,
calling you to remember
what is true
and enduring.

Journal Entry

I am done covering up my grief with being busy. I am done feeling "the hurry" race through my nervous system as a way to try to keep the grief at bay. I am done denying that my body must moan and pant, cry and shake. Grief will not leave me. She will not go away. She is now beating at the sides of my ribs. I have tried to push her away for so long now. I have seen her as the enemy and the source of my anxiety.

Yet now I see who she truly is. She is here to hold space for my freedom and for me to be birthed. She is not afraid of my sounds or wails. She can handle me losing it. I surrender and I feel her carrying me into the arms of the Beloved. And though I am tender and raw, I am okay. I know – I know in every fiber of my being – that death does not have the final word. And I feel your truth flow through me with such certainty: there is nothing that can separate me from you and in the end of it all, what remains is only Benevolence.

Prayer: God, I have tried to push away this grief for too long. You call me to let the holy wisdom of my body do what it must – what any hurt animal must do: cry out, moan, and shake. Remind me of how you are in my body, my grief, my longing, and my birthing.

Invitation: What would it be like to be guided by the holy wisdom of your body to do what it must do? And not just once, but for as often as you need for you to intuitively know the waves of grief have been honored within you? Often we need someone alongside to "hold space" for us. Please, find a trusted friend or healer to hold space for you. Know that you can contact me for Compassion Coaching.

Accept Support

I Talk, God Listens

Me: "I was in yoga class tonight and we were just about finished when the teacher had us lay on our backs, bend our knees, and bring the soles of our feet together. She suggested that we all put blocks under our knees for support. I was too tired and it felt good to stretch like this, so I didn't put the blocks under my knees. And then she came around and said, *'Hey mama, let yourself accept support!'* She put the blocks under my knees and I have to admit, it felt better and I could relax deeper. Her words stuck with me, *'Let yourself accept support'.*

"God, my life is about service. I care for others – from neighbors to clients, from my children to our larger community. I can get so wrapped up in my role as caregiver – of my children, of this world – that I forget to accept help. I forget to *ask* for support. Something in me shies away. I am so used to being the one "supporting" that I hardly ever ask for support from others. I'm even scared to now, God. I'm scared of rejection. I'm scared I'll be too needy. *I'm scared the support won't be there.*

"God, help me to ask for and accept support. Help me to be kind to myself as I feel vulnerable and shy. Help me to reach out. Keep offering me *your* support – keep telling me that *you* are the ultimate support and will always, always, always accept me just as I am and hold me for however long I need."

Prayer: God, it feels so vulnerable and raw to ask for support. Help me to be kind to myself as I try this out today.

Invitation: This week, what if you asked someone for support? It can be as simple as asking a friend to pick up your children at school so you can get to the gym, or go deeper and ask a dear one to "hold space" with you and listen to what's on your heart.

Letting the Responsible One Rest

Conversation

Me: "You know me; I tend to think I'm the one responsible for 'making it happen.' These tendencies are deeply woven within me. This is my default. But I hear you calling me to rest that 'Responsible One' within me. That's hard for me to do. Yet I know it is exactly what I need."

God: "Yep, you've got that right. I will accompany you. Let's let the 'Responsible One' rest for a bit. I know she is anxious. She feels like it's all up to her. And she does a lovely job of organizing and being in charge. Yet I can see how she is tired. I can see how there is a part of her that longs to rest. Let's offer her such rest today and this year, shall we, My Love?"

Me: "That's asking a lot! Yet, again, deep inside, the 'Responsible One' longs to rest. Okay, so let's let her rest a bit."

God: "And when she gets nervous and wonders how the other parts are doing and handling it all? Please, let's say some soothing words to her. Let's not pacify her. Let's regard her so she knows that we see her and her worries.

And that, yes, she does a great job at keeping it all together. We will check in with her and report back to her so she can actually rest. Okay?"

Me: "That sounds like a plan."

Prayer: Dear God, you know that I am such the "Responsible One." As I enter the holiday season, please keep whispering to me this week to just let her rest.

Invitation: As the holidays approach, listen to the deeper need of the "Responsible One" within you. See if she needs to rest. Speak soothing words to her and let her rest.

Forgiveness

Reflection

The holiday season is upon us, bringing with it get-togethers with family and dear ones. While there can be much joy in these gatherings, we can get triggered. Old memories of how we have been hurt and the ways we have hurt others can rise up in our minds and hearts. We might go into our old default mode of reacting, trying to protect our hearts. Ways we are currently hurting or causing hurt in our relationships can also come to light. The familiar anger, resentment, and shame that we carry with us can surface, dampening our joy and closing off our hearts.

Forgiveness is rarely something we talk about bringing into our everyday lives. The pace of our days keeps us busy, preventing us from ever giving attention to the hurts that inevitably happen in our relationships. Often our busyness is a way of deflecting what is painful. Yet left unattended, these hurts accumulate and impact how we relate to ourselves and our dear ones. They weave their way into our bodies, minds, and hearts – literally influencing our physiology, mood, and thoughts.

We avoid practicing forgiveness because we think the shame, anger, sadness or grief is too painful and will consume us if we bring these feelings to light. We may also think that forgiving ourselves or others is impossible – there's just too much there and it seems too heavy, too hard, and too complicated. We might believe that forgiveness means we condone what has happened and we will have to let go of healthy boundaries.

Yet, practicing forgiveness is true healing balm. When we learn to skillfully bring the light of mindfulness and compassion into our present moment, we find that such presence actually fortifies us. We see that our old ways of avoiding pain and protecting our hearts have left us weary and no closer to being truly happy. We discover that forgiveness in everyday ways opens and strengthens our hearts. We find ourselves able to stop running and finally feel a sense of peace. Clarity, wise action, and freedom arise. We feel more aligned with how we know we want to live.

Start with you. Forgive yourself. Let yourself off the hook. You've carried the memory of something you've done too long now, soul sister, on those precious shoulders of yours. Those harsh words you whisper to yourself every day keep you in perpetual penance.

There is a benevolent presence that holds all of this life. Whatever your creed, ultimately the last thing that remains is Love. Whether you believe in a god, many gods, an essence, or consciousness, it is benevolent. Total, complete understanding and regard. You belong to it.

When we embrace our goodness and remember that we belong to this benevolent forgiveness, light enters into every cell of our bodies. Clarity arises. We soften. We embody an inner sense of vitality. Our capacity to forgive others expands. We restore our sense of connection to everyone and everything.

Each time you say, "I see you. I forgive you," a space emerges. An abundance of light, sweetness, and delight fills you and spills out into the world. Your words with others become softer. Harsh judgment softens. Your very presence becomes a healing space for others to forgive their own selves.

Prayer: God, it is time I begin to forgive myself. May your Grace flow through me so I can see my innate goodness and feel your welcoming embrace. May my heart open, little by little, to forgive others.

Invitation: Forgiveness doesn't happen in one fell swoop. It takes time. This Advent season, consider devoting your attention to forgiveness. Begin with self-forgiveness in your daily life. Forgive yourself over and over again for the everyday ways you are human and "mess up." For not saying or doing the kind thing. For speaking harshly, ignoring, hurting, and turning away. Put your hand on that beautiful heart of yours and say, "I see you. I forgive you." And notice how the desire to practice forgiveness of others organically arises from your practice of self-forgiveness.

Tiny Gifts that Matter

Reflection

"Mommmmmmmmyyyyy," my three year old called to me to come into my bedroom. I was in a hurry, showering quickly, sighing as I put my hair up in a ponytail yet again, and worrying about getting out the door. In the first few seconds, I was annoyed she called me. But halfway through her plea, I heard it:

This is it, Lisa, a voice from within me said. *This is what matters. There's delight in her voice. Don't crush it or hurry it.*

"Mommy," she said, as I walked into the bedroom – exhaling, softening my shoulders, and relaxing my body. The first thing I saw was her little face filled with love and delight.

"Did you know?" she started singing. "Sometimes we hide pwesents for people we wuve and they have to find them!" She had made gifts and hid them while I was in the shower. "Now you have to go and find them!"

Bubbling with anticipation, eyes fully on me, and inviting me to join in her delight, she started to lead me to her hiding places for my gifts. One was on the small altar in our bedroom next to a candle and a statue of a woman deep in prayer reminding me that I need to pause there more often. One was tucked in my nightstand, on top of the box of notes I've kept from my husband over the years reminding me that we used to send love notes to each other all the time.

She tiptoed to the hiding spots and carefully, delightfully, gave me my gifts. They were wrapped in gently folded stationary from my former position at Georgetown – with all my credentials and title. I opened the first gift: two plastic bracelets.

"Your favorite color, Mommy! Turquoise!" my daughter exclaimed.

And I thought, *How beautiful that she knows this about me.* And I felt myself truly softening.

I opened the second gift: her precious fairy stickers.

I opened another gift: a picture. "I drew this for you. See, Mommy, it's you and you are smiling," she said as she pointed to the picture, looked up at me, and back at the picture again, showing me how it so closely resembles me.

I thank God that, a few minutes ago when she called me into the room, I didn't get annoyed.

I stood there on holy ground looking at my three year old – my flesh and blood – so full of generosity with tiny gifts filled with one desire: to delight my heart.

I held the picture in my hand. *She drew me smiling*, I thought.

It has taken me many years to realize that the tiny stuff matters. It has taken time for my nervous system to settle from those early years of being a new mom and really give myself permission to heal, be nourished, linger in the "holy now," and treasure the absolutely beautiful gift it is to be alive.

I often mess up. I yell. I come down punitively instead of building up positively. I sometimes get stressed and myopically focus on what doesn't matter. But I keep coming back to my devotion to delight, compassion, beauty, and connection. And that's only possible because I have spaciousness in my life now.

Several years ago, I decided to make some big changes based on what mattered most to us. And I realized something: I needed spaciousness – in mind, heart, day, and schedule.

I left my awesome, designed-for-me position at Georgetown University. I had tried to make it work – I analyzed, I got organized, I reorganized, I adjusted schedules, and I listened to soothing podcasts in the car to try to make my commute more tolerable. I did everything humanly possible to make it work. And then we faced the fact: it wasn't working.

That's when I surrendered to the truth within me that I could no longer deny. It was a huge risk. It was terrifying. But there comes a moment when you know what you have to do. And you do it.

Now, years later, I see the abundant blessings in my life because I chose to get out of the "daily grind" and give myself the space to notice the tiny gifts in my day. I began to do part-time consulting work with Georgetown University and other local organizations. I began to offer Compassion Coaching to readers of my blog all over the world. I reduced my hours to working mostly when our children are in school. And I love, love, love what I do.

I tell you honestly – I have spaciousness. I have a clearer mind. I have the energy to really *see* my children and be present with them. I've started to ease up on myself – and that means easing up on my dear ones. We have created a nourishing spaciousness that enables me to let go of harping on the small stuff and embrace the tiny things that matter.

The truth is that I was living with an amped up and stressed out nervous system. And when we walk around with these nervous systems holding old traumas and constantly overriding what our bodies know to do to heal, we are in a constant state of fight or flight, ready to explode or *implode*. Our attention is myopically focused on what's wrong. The small, messy stuff looks gigantic. We see the snow boots blocking the door, coats discarded and dropped on the floor, paint from art projects on the faucet knobs, clothes stained, rooms unorganized... and it makes us flip our lids. And the beautiful, quieter, delight-filled stuff gets trashed, dismissed, hurried, and overlooked.

But when we are resourced, we have abundance to offer instead of only morsels of patience, presence, and kindness.

It's time to be nourished down into every cell in our bodies. And yes, it is possible. It won't come from trying harder or finding a better way to be more organized.

It comes from learning how to nourish yourself throughout the day. It comes from taking responsibility for your mood, your "now," your health, your future, your response, your healing, and your life. It comes from naming what you need – to heal, to grieve, to have good friends in your life, and to have a voice. It comes from honoring what is most sacred to you, and often that means making some tough decisions.

And so when your daughter comes calling you – whether she is three or 13 – you can feel your feet on the earth, breathe into spaciousness, know what matters most, and *see* your daughter... and the hidden gifts – the obvious gifts, the not-so-pretty-and-in-disguise gifts, and the tiny beautiful gifts – and cherish them.

Prayer: God, help me to make the big and sometimes tough decisions that are aligned with what is most sacred to me so that I can see and be present to the tiny gifts that truly matter.

Invitation: As fall comes to an end soon, take time to discern what big decisions the Divine Within You might be asking you to make. Take time to linger in the tiny gifts of the season and allow these to open your heart to what deeply delights you.

Yes to the Mess

Yes to the mess of ribbon and
wrapping paper on the floor.
Yes to the perfect gift you picked out and
no one thanked you for.
Yes to the laughter and joy.
Yes to the quiet ache of loneliness still
lingering within you.
Yes to the "best china" and the plate breaking.
Yes to this being the last Christmas you
hold it all together.
Yes to finally sharing what's really going on.
Yes to the enmeshed mom who tries so hard,
the aloof dad,
the elephant in the room of addiction.
Yes to "better boundaries" and yes to having none.
Yes to the anxiety and your pursuit of perfection.
Yes to the hope in you,
the tiniest seed of calm growing in you.
Yes to the miscarriage,
the first holiday without your loved one,
the grief beating against your ribs,
the crying and the shaking.

Yes to fists pounding, feet kicking and stomping.
Yes to disturbing the silence.
Yes to losing it, yes to not being ready yet
and desperately trying to hold it all together.
Yes to "I'm not enough" and
yes to "Hell yes, I'm enough."
Yes to the camera breaking,
your heart silently breaking.
Yes to closing off your heart and
yes to opening it again.
Yes to the cool air against your face,
the smell of wood burning,
the moonlight over a silent night.
Yes to canceling your plans because
your child is sick and staying up all night.
Yes to not getting anything you really wanted and
yes to having it all.
Yes to resting.
Yes to not knowing, yes to uncertainty,
yes to having to wait,
yes to the knowing within you.
Yes to dropping the labels of "good" and "bad."
Yes to finally feeling the despair, disappointment,
shame and cupping your hands around your cheek.
Yes to the patterns you can't seem to get out of and
yes to starting again.
Yes to all the parts of you that you have rejected.
Yes to the hope, the light growing in you,
the strength rising within you.
Yes to welcoming it all with tenderness, saying,

"There is a place here at my table for you.
Please come.
Let's break bread together in this mess.
I no longer reject you. I love you.
Yes despair, yes half hopes,
yes imperfection, yes shame,
yes glorious light that keeps shining.
This is a holy mess
and I can't push you away any longer.
My God,
beyond all labels of 'good' or 'bad,'
each of you is a gift.
And I –
I am ready to finally be in the mess."

And now, Light illuminating everything,
the mud you stand in, your heart breaking,
your body trembling,
fully alive, raw, real, hands opening,
the only word you can utter
is "yes."

God Talks, I Listen

God: "Before time, I said yes. I said yes to existence. I said yes to the sun and moon. I said yes to stars and planets, galaxies and universes. I said yes to earth, water, fire, and air. I said yes to life – to plants, animals, and humans. I said yes to all that would come – including war and death, love, and birth.

"I said yes to you. And before you came into form, I asked if you wanted to say yes to this particular human experience – with all its complexity and beauty, suffering, and delight. And you said yes.

"I know it sounds crazy to say yes to heartache and suffering, dying, and death. In the biggest picture of your life, this being human thing is a gift. And each experience you have along the way is a gift. It may not seem like it. But I am alongside you as you have each experience and gently unwrap the gift that is life.

"There is a place at my table for all of it. Can you feel the surrender taking place in your whole body as you hear these words? Can you feel the 'letting go' of the tight ways you hold your jaw, shoulders, and belly?

"You and I together hold space for all that arises in this human experience with tenderness, kindness, and compassion. *That* is why we say yes to it all. You and I together breathe with the feelings of joy, disappointment, anger, love, grief, loneliness, delight, and happiness. You and I together hold space for the waves of thoughts to rise and dissolve without reacting. You and I together hold space for the sensations of tightness, spaciousness, openness, constriction, and freedom to be felt – not pushing away or holding on – just experienced.

"This is freedom. I know it's a radical posture to take, My Love. But gradually, I see how you are dropping into this wisdom and feeling the inner freedom that comes from saying yes to it all. I sense the powerful thanksgiving budding in your heart. I've heard your prayers of gratitude for every single moment of your life. *Yes!* Oh, this human existence you have said yes to – it's all just for you to experience it and, if you choose, to feel Me beside you and hear Me whispering, 'Let's let this life be one big delight, shall we'?"

Prayer: God, I feel you beside me inviting me to this radical way of living where I push nothing out of my present moment experience, but rather I learn to gently say yes and welcome what arises to my table of awareness with kindness and compassion.

Invitation: When you are suffering in any way, put your hand on your heart, and gently say yes to the sensations, thoughts, and emotions as they come, without judgment or pushing them away. Create spaciousness to allow what is here to be here. Start with the "smaller" sufferings in life before moving to the bigger ones.

And when you are experiencing delight or a deep sense of connection, put your hand on your heart, and gently say yes to the sensations, thoughts, and emotions as they come, without gripping them or trying to keep them. Create spaciousness to savor this moment. Offer a prayer of gratitude for being in this human experience. And notice how it draws you closer to a sense of delight and connection with the Beloved.

A Sacred Revolution

Alongside the Beloved

"What do I have to do?" I asked.
"Nothing," God said.
"What do I have to fear?" I asked.
"Nothing," God said.
So I exhaled,
took the Beloved's hand,
and leaped.

Reflection

The other morning, I woke up early before anyone else. It's my sacred space to be in the darkness, watching the sun rise, listening to the whispers of the Beloved within me that are clearer in the quiet of the morning than in the hustle and bustle of the day. I'm lying on the couch and writing by the white lights of our Christmas tree.

I hear it. I sense it – within me and so many others. There's a fire growing, a wave forming, a revolution of the heart-body-mind-spirit rising. I have been hearing this call to rise, risk, and leap. Yesterday morning I asked, "What do I have to do?"

"Nothing," God said.

"What do I have to fear?" I asked.

"Nothing," God said again.

I don't even have to fear failure. I can't fail. I don't even have to fear not being enough or doing enough. I'm already enough. And any expression of the Sacred Aliveness within me that I open to is enough.

"You see," the Beloved said, "failure is impossible."

And so, I felt myself take the hand of the Beloved... and leap.

There is a growing devotion to this Truth within me. There is a growing sense of calm and confidence with turning toward this call of the Beloved Within – regardless of what the world thinks or how the world reacts.

I believe this is the spiritual call of a lifetime: to hear the wild invitation of the Beloved that we know as Truth, and risk following what we hear. To remember we cannot fail. To remember we don't have to *do* anything. To remember that the Divine only wants to be alongside us, accompanying us. To remember what the mystics and sages, like Rumi and Hafiz, have been saying for centuries: God is all about delight.

Risk answering the invitation.

Risk living your life based on what is most sacred to you.

Risk delight.

Risk following what delights your heart.

The world will pull at you, distract you, and vie for your attention. From the moment we wake up, there are a hundred things just on our way to the kitchen that could distract us from what is most sacred to us and what delights our hearts. The world spins us into hurry. It pulls us into numbing out and self-doubt. It pulls our attention away from who matters most. A day, a year or a lifetime can go by without us ever really living according to what is sacred and what deeply delights our heart.

But when you pause and listen – when you cultivate this skillful habit of "showing up" *as you are* in the presence of the Beloved – you'll *know* what is most sacred to you. You'll *know* the deep delights of your heart. You'll stretch out your hand to the world, fingers spread wide, and say, "Not now, world. Not this moment."

And you will turn your attention to embrace this precious life of yours with a radical focus and devotion. And you will take the hand of the Beloved and take "the next right step." And you will leap.

And your presence – a presence that is aligned with your truth – will inspire your dear ones, your community, and your world. Not your quest for perfection. Not your tidy and neat life. But rather your faith in jumping into the unknown, embracing all the perfectly imperfect parts of you – shadows and light. And you will be a healing presence for this world. This is a sacred revolution – of our hearts, families, lives, and world.

Prayer: Dear God, as this year comes to an end, I hear the call to gently leap. Leap into trust. Leap into delight. Leap into risking. Leap into following what you whisper to me in the quiet on these cold, dark mornings. I am embracing this precious life of mine by taking your hand and leaping into the unknown.

Invitation: This week, before the new year begins, take some time to play with these words: *leap*, *risk*, and *trust*. Weave them into your day, reminding yourself that you really don't have to "do" anything except take the hand of the Beloved. This is a sacred revolution bound to liberate your heart and our world.

Conclusion

A True Happiness

You have panted for rest –
to discover a place where
you can finally feel whole.

You have gone out looking
for happiness in places that
have left you empty, anxious
and alone

only to return
to the inner landscape
of your heart

and discover that
the source of your happiness
lies within.

Now the wine doesn't seem so appealing,
the long work days for the big house and
vacations seem nuts,
and turning away again and again
from the ones who matter most
seems foolish.

You put down your cell phone,
turn off the mind-numbing violent crime show,
put away the box of cookies you were about to finish off,

and you sit.

Your stuff is still here
but the regret, grief, and fear
that seemed so scary to face –
like they would surely overtake you –
now are waves
and you feel them
as tears of truth
finally being breathed
as they wet your cheeks.

You find that the waves settle,
and you are still here.
You feel your pulse, your breath.

That's when you sense it – a deep peace within you.
Here all along, it has waited for you, been within you,
calling you to rest.
Beyond names or words, you know it as you.

This is where you know that you are good,
you belong, you are enough,
and anything else is pure myth –
something you learned a long time ago
from others who were hurting, too.

Spaciousness now swims across your chest.
You soften. You rest.
The deep peace that dwells within
welcomes you Home.

The snow is gently falling as I write these lines. Christmas is over and the new year is arriving soon. I'm up early. The house is quiet. Our puppy is at my feet, my constant companion in this writing journey. I pull a warm blanket around my shoulders. I can still sense the impulse to hurry and get things done before everyone wakes up. But instead of getting wrapped up in the hurry, I put my hand on my heart and say, "Of course I'd feel this. It's okay, Love." I've come to experience these words as healing balm that I use to gently massage my heart and nerves. As I say them, I feel myself begin to settle and soften.

There are times my old habits still call to me – to strive, to think it's all up to me, and to "go out there" looking for happiness. But I don't want to go around panting for rest or scrounging for peace. "Come inside," the Beloved calls.

Just as I felt it on that cold, rainy day with my infant in the stroller, I can feel the Beloved's hand reaching out to me in this moment. "There's another way, Love. Come, let's do this together," I hear. And I can choose to take the hand of the Beloved to come inside to my own heart and rest.

The gems I've shared here in this book have been my lived-out response to taking the Beloved's hand in the messy and miraculous of everyday life. Over the years, I have learned to pause – not always and not "perfectly" – but often enough that I can hear the Beloved calling to me through the myriad voices within and around me.

And I can bring compassion into my experience of the present moment. I can hold space for my own self as an inner vastness welcomes me Home. I can hear the beating of my own heart. I can choose to go gently. I can choose to linger. And I can feel my divine feminine power rising as I align my decisions with what is most sacred to me and what deeply delights my heart. For I have discovered that the deepest delights of my heart are God's deepest delights. And like my favorite mystical poet, Hafiz, writes: "God is all about delight and only wants to join us and dance."

I pray that...

> ...in sharing some of my personal journal entries, conversations with God, and reflections that you, too, can feel the Beloved's presence whose hand is always outstretched to you.

> ...as you pause and "listen within," you come to know what deeply delights your heart and you feel a God of Compassion accompanying you in each season of your life to embody those delights.

> ...as you practice self-compassion, you awaken a strong, feminine power within you to align your everyday life with what is most sacred to you – in the big and little moments of your day.

> ...our compassionate presence will inspire others to connect to the Beloved within them, follow what delights their own hearts, and align their lives with what is most sacred to them.

...together we will encourage each other to let our light shine.

This is how we transform our hearts, homes, and world! This is what happens when we risk delight!

About the Author

Photo credit: David S. Spence

Lisa McCrohan is a somatic psychotherapist and compassion coach in private practice who has worked for over 20 years in the world of wellness at universities, nonprofits, churches, and counseling centers. She holds Master's degrees in clinical social work and in pastoral ministry from Boston College and advanced trainings in mindfulness, trauma recovery, and yoga. Her writing has been featured at Upworthy.com and GUWellness, Georgetown University's wellness program for faculty and staff. She lives in Maryland with her husband and two children.

Visit the author at LisaMcCrohan.com

Made in the USA
Lexington, KY
27 April 2017